George Kell

Hello Everybody, I'm George Kell

George Kell
with
Dan Ewald

SPORTS PUBLISHING
Champaign IL 61820

Production Director: Susan M. McKinney
Dustjacket and photo insert design: Julie L. Denzer

ISBN:1-57167-180-3

SPORTS PUBLISHING
804 N. Neil
Champaign, IL 61820

Printed in the United States

DEDICATION

Where do I start to thank all the people who have been part of my life? My parents, of course, who were there for me all the time as I chased my dream.

My wife of 50 years, Charlene, who died of cancer in 1991. She raised our two children, often alone, while I was away.

My children, George, Jr. and Terrie, who do not remember too much about my baseball career because they were so young. But they do remember their daddy was gone from home a long time. They and my grandchildren live only 20 and 30 miles from Swifton. We are very close as a family.

Terrie has taken her mother's place—hostess at Christmas time. George, Jr., a gourmet cook, entertains all the family at Thanksgiving.

To Carolyn, my wife of four years, who came into my life at the right time. She is truly family. My children love her. They encourage the romance and the marriage.

I don't want to forget my lone brother, Skeeter, who played in the major leagues for a short time. He relished and supported me throughout my career. He is a very successful businessman today. He and his wife, Sue, have been married for 50 years. They have raised four wonderful children—and I love them as if they were my own.

And certainly my thanks to the city of Swifton and all the people who have supported me in everything I've done. We all grew up here so poor, but didn't know it because everyone was poor in those days.

Thanks to Senator Dale Bumpers. We are almost like brothers. He gave the eulogy at Charlene's funeral and I know how hard it was for him.

How can I thank Dan Ewald, my close friend and confidant? He convinced me to write this book when I really didn't want to. Now I'm so glad I did. My whole life is in print forever.

Dan spent three days in Swifton. He saw my church, my school, my automobile agency and my farmland. Most of all, he met the good people here.

Now he knows why I have never left here and never will. Dan, thanks for coming.

—*George Kell*

CONTENTS

Foreword vi
Acknowledgments viii

1   Home Sweet Swifton 1
2   Tough Times, Good Times 7
3   Always There 15
4   A Turn in the Road 21
5   "My, My" Mr. Mack 27
6   The War Years 33
7   Hello Detroit 41
8   The Perfect Place to Be 49
9   Breaking the Color Barrier 57
10 Confidence and a Cup of Coffee 67
11 The Green Monster and Ted 75
12 The Golden Years 81
13 Almost in the Dugout 91
14 It Was Just Time 99
15 Behind the Mike and Talking to Casey 105
16 Hello, Detroit . . . Again 111
17 "Hello Everybody . . . I'm George Kell" 119
18 The Year of the Tiger 127
19 The Second Time Around 137
20 Almost There 145
21 No More Like Jim 149
22 Spanning Six Decades 155
23 Time and Change 163
24 Business After Baseball 169
25 She Was a Lady 179
26 Another Prayer Answered 187
27 Again . . . It Was Time 191
28 A Time to Share 195
29 And Swifton's Still the Same 201
30 George Kell Remarks 205
31 We'll Never Forget 209

FOREWORD

By Dale Bumpers
United States Senator

It was a typically hot July day in 1970 when I met George Kell, who had long been an icon in Arkansas. He had retired from major league baseball while with the Orioles and returned to his beloved Swifton, Arkansas, a small community of about 850 souls in the northeastern part of the state. I was a "he hasn't got a chance" candidate for Governor at the time, and a friend of mine in nearby Newport, a much larger community where George owned an automobile agency, had invited 10-12 local opinion-makers to meet this unknown candidate, who, according to the polls, stood at a whopping 4% of the vote in the Democratic Primary.

We gathered around a table in a side dining room of the most popular eatery in Newport and I made my pitch. I knew George could make a significant difference in my campaign if I could persuade him to get involved, so I aimed my remarks at him primarily. He said little, just as he has said little all his life, but we "connected" that day and have remained connected ever since, partly because of just plain chemistry and partly because we both loved baseball, both were devout Methodists, both farmed, both doted on our families and both were committed to a more vibrant and prosperous Arkansas.

George had never before involved himself in a political campaign, but in a quiet, dignified way, he became a major force in my campaign that catapulted me into the Arkansas Governor's office and later the U. S. Senate. Baseball fans the nation over would have been shocked to know that George was exuberantly involving himself in politics, but they would have nodded knowingly on seeing his determination and commitment. As one of baseball's all-time great clutch hitters, he sure came through in the clutch for me.

If I were the only person whose life had been changed so dramatically by George Kell, this anecdote would be unimpressive, but countless others have also had their lives enriched in so many different ways by this truly remarkable man whose native intellect, appealing reserve and total commitment to Judeo-Christian values is so rare.

His return to Swifton may be unfathomable to some, but to those of us who have been long-time "Kell-watchers", it was as predictable as his regular attendance at the tiny Methodist Church where he was a lay leader, member of the choir and taught a Sunday School class.

Once in the Governor's office, I offered George a position on the State Highway Commission, one of the most prestigious positions an Arkansas Governor can bestow; he quickly said no. He said he was too busy, but, in truth, he was afraid people would think he was "cashing in" on our friendship. Not until his fellow townsmen pleaded, cajoled and begged did he yield and take the ten-year appointment. Next to baseball, I think George enjoyed his tenure more than anything he's ever done. He is considered one of the best members ever to serve on the Commission.

Despite the fame, honors and glory that have come his way, this self-effacing and amazing man has never deviated from the principles instilled in him by his mother and father, to whom he was totally devoted. *Hello Everybody, I'm George Kell* is long overdue. Few people have been honored so lavishly in so many ways, so many times and his real character manifests itself in the fact that he never felt he deserved any of it.

When the publisher of this book called and asked me to write this short foreword, I rushed to get my Roget's Thesaurus out, but even it didn't have enough superlatives to fully describe George Kell. Crossword puzzle aficionados know that the answer to the clue, "A-one" or "top notch" is almost always "oner". George Kell is a "oner". When you finish this book you will understand why.

ACKNOWLEDGMENTS

George Kell and Dan Ewald would like to acknowledge all the wonderful characters which baseball has generously shared with all of us. It is impossible to individually acknowledge all who have contributed so much to enrich so many lives. For all who have, though, we extend our most sincere thanks. You will forever remain in our hearts and in our prayers. We particularly wish to acknowledge the assistance and support of Baseball's Hall of Fame. There is no greater shrine of athletic excellence.

CHAPTER ONE

HOME SWEET SWIFTON

"If they hit the ball to George, he simply catches it and throws the runner out."　　　　　　　　—Clyde Kell, 1934

Там There were two movie theaters on Main Street when I was growing up in Swifton, Arkansas. They stood right across the street from each other. We'd walk up a few blocks into what we called downtown. For a nickel or a dime we'd catch a matinee on Saturday before heading to the park to play a pick-up game.

The town seemed so big back then. Besides the theaters, we had two barber shops, three or four grocery stores and a handful of other little shops. Downtown really wasn't more than about three blocks running up and down Main Street just east of the railroad tracks.

On Saturday nights, though, those three blocks were crammed with almost everyone who lived in Swifton. It didn't matter what age you were. Come Saturday night, it was time to spiffy up and just sort of hang around downtown.

They were good times.

My daddy had bought me a used bicycle from one of the neighbors up the street. I used to rent it out on Saturday nights to a kid who would come into town from the country.

That boy loved to ride that bicycle more than anything in the world. His daddy worked a farm and all the helpers shopped at the company store. I never got any money from the boy, but he'd always give me a pair of socks or a shirt for letting him use my bicycle. Every Saturday, I told him to be real careful with it. I needed that bicycle all week to deliver my paper route.

On a map, Swifton isn't much more than a speck. On some maps, in fact, it doesn't even show up. Swifton sits 18 miles northeast of Newport and 40 miles southwest of Walnut Ridge in Arkansas. Alicia, just north up Interstate 67, is the closest marker. That highway runs right alongside the railroad tracks and pretty much splits the town in half.

Even back in those days, I-67 was a busy highway. When we were little kids, we'd watch all the big trucks roll up and down that highway. We used to dream about where those trucks were coming from and where they were going. We wondered if we would ever get to see some of those places where those trucks had been. I-67 is still a main truck route between Dallas and St. Louis. It's a lot better paved and the trucks have gotten bigger.

Back when I was a youngster and right up through today, Swifton stays at just about one thousand people. There's a town meeting hall, a corner grocery store and a spanking new post office on Main Street now; although there's not much of a downtown anymore. All the people now own cars. They can get anything or do anything they want to now by driving down to Newport or going over to Jonesboro just about 40 miles to the east.

That's about all that has changed in the town over the last 70 years, though. A lot of my old friends have passed on, but most of their families still live in Swifton. I can't say that I know everybody in town by name, but everyone sort of knows everyone else by sight. Or at least that's the way it seems. That's a pretty good feeling that no amount of money can buy.

I'm a very fortunate man. I can walk up and down the streets all around Swifton and bump into so many warm memories and remember so many good times. I can still walk to the same church I went to when I was a youngster. The cemetery where my first wife, Charlene, my mother and father and my brother, Frank are all buried is just across the railroad tracks on the west side of I-67.

The high school is new, but I can walk a couple of blocks from my house and look out over the field where we played so many pick-up baseball games. For a special treat, I can jump into my car and drive about 15 minutes to the north side of Newport. About a stone's throw west of the highway sits George Kell Park, with a collection of lighted baseball diamonds, a swimming pool and picnic areas.

The American Legion teams play all of their games at George Kell Park now. The city named it after me when I was elected to the Baseball Hall of Fame in 1983.

For different types of topography, Arkansas is a treasure chest. It's got something to satisfy almost any appetite. Up in the northwest corner of the state are the Boston Mountains. Down toward the west central sector are the Ouachita Mountains. There are hills and valleys all around Little Rock and Hot Springs.

Swifton is smack in the northeast section of the state and flatter than a carpenter's rule. It's got some of the most beautiful farm land that God ever created. Anybody visiting Swifton better get used to the mosquitoes, though. They go along with the territory of a well watered-down rice field.

There are a variety of crops—soybeans, wheat, corn. But those rice fields, coupled with the sticky summer heat, breed a batch of mosquitoes that can sometimes test the nerves of even the oldest Swifton native. For me, those mosquitoes are a small price to pay for the luxury of living in my hometown.

About 80 percent of the Swifton economy is based on farming. These are real people here. They know the land. They appreciate the earth. They don't need much. They work hard, raise their families and pretty much all go to church together. They're grateful for every little blessing they have.

One of the things I'm most proud of is that I've lived every day of my life in Swifton, Arkansas. I've had to spend baseball seasons in various cities across the United States, and I've appreciated the special features of each city and all of the people who have treated my family and me so beautifully for so many years. But once the season was finished, or when I was broadcasting and a game was over, I got myself back to Swifton quicker than one of our mosquitoes can stick a stinger into your left arm.

Sometimes making a connection was a little bit of a hassle. Obviously, there are no flights into Swifton. The closest stop is Little Rock, which is about a two-hour drive from home. The reward was well worth the trouble. I was going home to Swifton.

I've got to be the luckiest man on the face of the earth. I've pretty much been able to realize almost every dream I've had in life. I wanted to become a big league ball player and I played in the major leagues for 15 seasons. I wanted to make it into the Hall of Fame, and in 1983 that dream came true. After my playing career was finished, I wanted to become the best baseball announcer I could possibly be. And I was able to live that dream for 38 years.

I've been fortunate to have traveled all over the United States. Doors have been opened to me that I never even thought I'd be able to knock on. But I'm so proud that I've kept my home in Swifton. And it'll stay that way till the day I die.

It's sort of funny how people choose their homes. Some people want to leave home and try another part of the country, but never get the chance to leave the place where they were born. Others get bounced around because of their jobs. Sometimes they just sort of get settled into a place when they have to pack up for the next stop. Businessmen feel more comfortable in a big city. Professors feel more at home in a college town.

For me, that feeling of walking down the street knowing that everybody in town shares pretty much the same values as I do is the real definition of home. I've had the opportunity to choose wherever I wanted to live anywhere in the United States. But I was raised in Swifton. This is where my mother and daddy planted values in me that I still practice today. This is where I raised my children. This is where I've gone to the same church ever since I was a kid. I learned to play ball here. I learned to work and how to sweat hard at a job here. I've learned how to appreciate every gift that God has given me right here. Everything that I hold valuable in life started right here in Swifton. To this very day, nothing has changed. Not in Swifton and not in me.

I've spent a lot of time trying to put together all the pieces and figure out why I've been so blessed. When you're playing ball for a living, you don't take the time to really understand how lucky you are. You're too busy worrying about facing guys like Bob Feller and Bob Lemon to think about anything but trying to hit that ball on the nose.

When I was broadcasting, I worked as hard as I did when I was a player to become the same type of professional in the booth as I was on the field. It never occurred to me how many people I might be touching through my broadcast on any given night. It finally struck me after I had to call it quits in the winter of 1997.

I had reached a point where I could no longer physically do the Tiger broadcasts. I could still call the games; I still love baseball and broadcasting as much as I ever did. But after my back operation, I wasn't able to move around and do the kind of traveling that the job demands.

When I retired, though, I honestly felt that hardly anyone back up in Detroit would notice the difference. I always tried to do a professional job without taking myself too seriously.

Shortly after I made the announcement of my retirement, Joe Falls wrote a column in *The Detroit News* suggesting that fans write a get well letter and send it to me in Swifton.

I couldn't believe the response I received. I must have gotten about 300 letters. They all wished me well and told me how much they would miss me on the broadcasts. I read each one of them. I saved each one. Some day I'm going to put them in my scrapbook because they mean that much to me.

Everybody I've talked to and all the letters I received have been so kind. I had never even dreamed that I had touched so many people.

Some of the letters said, "We knew summer truly had started when we heard your voice." Others said, "George, we're going to miss that sweet voice...we've gone to sleep many nights watching the Tigers with you and it will never be the same without you."

My wife, Carolyn, cried when we read some of those letters. I couldn't hold back all of my tears. I truly never realized that people cared so much.

All I ever tried to do with my broadcasts was to tell the story about the game going on out on the field. I tried to tell it with the honesty and decency that was bred into me ever since I was a boy and with the insight of somebody who happened to be very lucky in the game.

It all began in Swifton. And I'm so grateful to God and my family that I have been able to spend my entire life in the one place that I really feel is home.

CHAPTER TWO

TOUGH TIMES, GOOD TIMES

Except for what people read in history books, hardly anyone remembers what the Depression was really like. Even growing up during the Depression, I really never knew how tough things were. When you grow up during a Depression, you just naturally assume that's the way things are supposed to be.

We were poor. Nearly everyone in Swifton was poor. We didn't eat fancy meals, but we always had enough to eat. Our clothes were old, but my mother always kept us neat. Nobody really gave much thought to this thing called a Depression.

I remember I was always happy just to play baseball and basketball. If I had an extra quarter or fifty cents in my pocket, I was rich. I felt just like John Rockefeller.

My mother, my father, my two brothers and I never complained about not having certain things. We simply all pitched in to keep things going and I remember having a very enjoyable boyhood.

I had three different jobs to help do my share for the Kell household. In the morning before school, I'd get up early and deliver the *Arkansas Democrat* on my bicycle. As I said, the railroad pretty much splits the town in half, and my route covered the lower end of town. My brother, Frank, had the upper.

I delivered wood every day to these two doctors in town. They had a big stove in their office that burned logs for heat. Besides logs, they also needed a regular supply of kindling wood, and I had to make a regular delivery to them every day after school before I could play ball.

We had two milk cows in those days. I'd milk one and my brother, Skeeter, would milk the other. We'd bring the milk to my mother and she would somehow strain it. Then, later in the evening, my brothers and I would go around town delivering milk to the dozen customers we had.

I got that bicycle I loved so much when I was about 12 years old. My daddy gave it to me for Christmas. It was a used bicycle that he had bought for about three dollars from one of the families in town. That bicycle wasn't all in one piece when daddy bought it, but he made sure he collected all the pieces.

It wasn't until many years later that I fully appreciated what my daddy had to go through to buy that bicycle for me. It had to be embarrassing for him to go up into another man's attic and gather up all the parts so that he could put together an old bicycle for his son. I drove that bicycle around town so proudly like it was brand new and straight out of the Sears & Roebuck catalog. I loved that old bicycle. I appreciate it even more today when I look back on how daddy had to sacrifice to get it.

We lived in three different houses in Swifton before my parents were finally able to buy one right at the east edge of downtown. That house was the first one we ever lived in that had running water and a bathroom inside. There was an old outhouse in the backyard, and I remember one time I went out to use it because I had completely forgotten that we finally had inside plumbing.

This was back in the heart of the Depression. It was tough on daddy and my mother. Not once did they ever complain or feel sorry for themselves. They did the best they could on limited resources. And they did doggone good.

More important than anything to daddy and mother—even more important than baseball to daddy—was church. My parents were members of the Swifton United Methodist Church. It's the same church—in fact, the same building—of which I'm still a member today.

Daddy was a religious man. I mean deeply religious. It wasn't that false kind of religion that you see in some people. Daddy never went around just preaching religion. He practiced being a Christian. He didn't just give you lip service.

When the door of that church opened, he was there. He was Sunday School superintendent, chairman of the official board, lay leader and he also taught a Sunday School class.

Not so many years ago, I was asked to address a group of senior citizens in Detroit. I told them that I am very proud of my baseball and broadcasting accomplishments. But the one thing that makes me happier than anything else is the fact that I succeeded my father in every one of those positions he held in our church.

Daddy was so proud when I made it into the Baseball Hall of Fame. But he was more proud of the fact that I had followed his footsteps in our church. That meant so much to daddy. And it means even more to me.

Church has always been a very important part of my life. If I wasn't out of town playing a game or broadcasting a game, I can never remember a Sunday in my life where I wasn't at the Swifton United Methodist Church for Sunday morning services.

Even when I was just a kid, I loved going to church. What I liked about it when I was young is that it gave me the chance to put on my best clothes. I only had but one set, but that one set was the best Sunday-go-to-church outfit anyone had seen. I walked into that church like I had just walked off Madison Avenue.

I was proud of that outfit I wore. I wanted all the people to look at me.

I was the ring leader of some kids my age. Like all kids, we were prone to get into a little trouble. I had to face the music one time for accidentally popping off some fireworks in the back of the church. But I loved going to services. To this day, I don't believe I treasure anything more.

My daddy's name was Clyde Kell. My mother's name was Alma. They're both gone to heaven now. They came from Imboden, Arkansas, about 40 miles from Swifton.

Daddy was a barber and also was a pitcher on what was called the Swifton Town Team. They played various other town teams around the area. The Swifton team would hire daddy to come to town from Imboden to pitch once or twice a week.

Daddy was good. He was the best pitcher in the whole area and became the star of the team. Finally one day, the leaders of the team propositioned him.

"Mr. Kell, if you will move to Swifton, we'll buy you a barber shop and put you into business here," they said. "Then you can play ball for us all the time and we'll pay you for that, too."

This was around 1920. My parents had recently married and none of us boys had yet come along. So they agreed to the deal and the Kells have been a part of Swifton ever since. I was born in

1922. My brother Frank was born in 1924, and my youngest brother Skeeter was born in 1929. Skeeter grew up to play professional baseball. He made it to the Philadelphia Athletics for the 1952 season and part of 1953.

Daddy had a fastball that the hitters could only hear as it whistled by. He had a good breaking pitch to set up his fastball and knew how to get both of them over the plate. More than anything else, daddy knew all of the little ins and outs of the game. And, man, how he did love to play. I think that next to me, daddy was the most fanatical person about baseball that I ever knew.

When my parents moved to Swifton, the Fourth of July Picnic was one of the town's biggest celebrations of the year. Today those picnics are a little bit different.

Back in those days, the highlight of the picnic was a doubleheader between the Town Team and one from a visiting town. This was serious stuff. The whole town turned out to cheer for these games. Daddy would pitch one game and then play outfield in the next one. He made $300 for the day.

"That's more money than I ever had at one time," he once told me. "That's more money than I could make in a month of barbering. Back then I was lucky to make $40 or $50 a week."

Daddy could have played ball at a much higher level. He was good enough to play professionally. Back then, though, they didn't pay that much money to play in the minor leagues.

What really convinced him to stick with his scissors and comb was that he was not prepared to leave his family for the amount of time professional baseball demands. He figured that between barbering and playing for the Town Team that he could make ends meet. As long as he could play ball at some level, daddy was happy.

I loved going to the park and watching him play. When I was only about eight years old, I'd grab an old glove that he had given me and go out before games to field grounders and shag flies. I loved to play with the older men because I knew it was a challenge.

I was twelve when we played Tuckerman. That's a small town between Swifton and Newport. Tuckerman was always our biggest rival. I was serving as batboy and we put a whipping on them that year. We had a 10-0 lead in the ninth inning with daddy pitching. I got the shock of my young life just before the last of the ninth inning started.

"Get your glove and go ahead out to second base to finish the game," daddy told me.

I couldn't believe my ears. I was so tickled I almost jumped clear out of my shoes. I felt just like some Hall of Famer trotting out to my position to start that last half inning. Nothing was hit to me, but I was so proud to be standing out on that field with my daddy pitching.

My mother almost hit the roof of our old car, though, on our ride back to Swifton. She turned to daddy and looked him square in the eye.

"I wish you would tell me one thing, Clyde Kell," she said in a tone that hung somewhere between anger and disbelief. "What in the world were you thinking when you put my son out there on the field with those grown men?

"That boy might have been killed right on the spot. What in the world do you think might have happened if one of those men had hit a shot straight at his face?"

Daddy just sat there for a moment before calmly giving his simple reply.

"He would have caught it," he said. "If they hit the ball to George, he simply catches it and throws the runner out."

Years later when I played in the major leagues and would sometimes have to move in at third base against some power hitter, I would stand there and smile to myself. I'd think about what daddy said that day—"If they hit the ball to George, he simply catches it and throws the runner out."

There was never a time in my life that I didn't think about playing baseball. I loved the game. I loved every part about it.

Both of my brothers loved baseball, but I think I was more fanatical about it than anybody. In fact, I don't think there was any kid in town who ate and slept the game as much as I did.

I followed the major leaguers as closely as I could. I read all the boxscores in the newspaper every day. I knew every player and all of their averages. When I played on the fields, I used to pretend I was one of my real-life heroes.

The St. Louis Cardinal games were broadcast over the radio into Swifton. Everybody in Swifton loved the Cardinals because St. Louis is only about 250 miles north.

There were the Dean Brothers. Jim Bottomley played first base. Frankie Frisch played second and Pepper Martin was at third. Leo Durocher was the shortstop.

My Aunt Ethel and Aunt Addie lived up in St. Louis. One worked at the Mark Twain Hotel and the other worked at the Mayfair, three blocks up the street. Each summer I'd go up to St. Louis and stay a week. They had enough pull at the hotels to get me Knothole Gang passes so that I could go to the Cardinal games for free.

I'd sit down the left field line and think this is what heaven must be. I loved playing ball with all my friends in Swifton, but when I sat out in those seats in old Sportsman's Park, I didn't want those days ever to end.

I enjoyed playing the field, running the bases or just shagging flies before a game. There was nothing in the world like swinging a bat, though. Hearing that crack of the bat and seeing a line drive fall safely in front of an outfielder was the greatest feeling in the world. I don't know why, but hitting always seemed to come easy to me.

When we got our chores done after school, we would go over to the park to play pick-up games. We didn't always have enough for two full teams, so we'd split up and fill in the best we could. I really didn't mind it, because fewer players meant more times up at bat.

Because I could hit and field a little better than most kids my age, I generally was the center of attention. When I was 14 years old, the state held a tournament in northeast Arkansas. The Swifton Town team qualified because my father was such a good pitcher. By that time, I was also playing shortstop for the Town Team. The kids' team I played for also qualified for the tournament in its own division.

We played the kids' games in the morning and won the tournament. I played shortstop and won a glove for being named Most Valuable Player of the tournament.

The men's tournament was played in the afternoon. We took that to the championship round, but lost in the final game. In spite of that loss, I was named Most Valuable Player for that division and wound up winning a second glove.

We were poor, but we were never short of baseball mitts in the Kell household after that tournament.

I played baseball throughout high school. I loved it more than anything, but basketball was a bigger sport at our school. Everything seemed to center around basketball.

Not everybody played baseball. That's why I started playing with the grown-ups because they played more. I wanted to play as much as I could and so by the time I was 15, I was probably a little better than the average player around the whole area.

I wasn't the greatest nor the worst student, but I enjoyed going to school. I got involved with everything. If they had a class play, I was in it. If there was some sort of special celebration, I volunteered to participate. I got smack dab into the middle of everything. I really enjoyed working with all the kids and the teachers.

People weren't jealous of me or anything like that, but I did become the focus of attention in basketball and baseball because sports came naturally to me. I played forward in basketball; I wasn't that good, but I was a take-charge sort of guy, so they named me captain.

My family always had to scuffle to get by financially. In my senior year, the principal told me he was going to give me a letter "S" with a star on it because I was captain of the basketball team. There was one little catch. The school had given me the letter but it was up to the individual to get his own jacket.

"How much do they cost?" I asked him. He told me $5.

I was so excited I must have flown home to tell my parents. Daddy wanted me to have the jacket but told me there was no way we had an extra $5 to buy a new one.

A couple of days later, my mother stopped me before I went to school.

"How long before they need that $5?" she asked. I told her about six weeks.

"Go ahead and order it," she said. "I'll come up with the money somehow by then."

And she did. She saved a nickel here and a dime there from grocery money and from the money she earned doing all of her work. When the state decided to pave I-67 that ran through the town, my mother picked up extra money by washing clothes for the work crew.

I was so proud of that jacket I wore it every day for as long as I can remember. It didn't matter how hot it was outside. I was too proud of it to take it off.

That's the way it always was in our home. We never had much money. But we always had everything we needed. I believe that's pretty much the way it's always been in Swifton.

It's also one of the reasons I've always felt like I've been one of the richest men in the world.

CHAPTER THREE

ALWAYS THERE

E ven after I—and a little later Skeeter—got to the big leagues, daddy never went around bragging about us. If you didn't ask him, you would have never known that he had two sons playing in the major leagues. Bragging wasn't his way. He was a quiet man.

Every once in a while I'd bump into a traveling salesman who might call on his barber shop or run into him in Swifton.

"I used to go into the shop and talk to Clyde about baseball," one of them told me. "You were playing for the Tigers and leading the league in hitting at the time. I'd say 'How's George doing?' He was real polite and might say 'Oh, he got a couple of more hits last night.' That's all he'd say. He never brought it up. And he never bragged."

That's the way daddy was. He was confident and content. It was his dream to have his three sons play baseball in the major leagues. Two of us made it. My brother, Skeeter, played for the Philadelphia Athletics in 1952. If Frank hadn't been killed in the service during World War II maybe daddy would have realized his entire dream.

But daddy was not a braggart. He was happy and proud of us in his own way. He never needed to go around bragging. He was the kind of guy who truly let his actions speak for him.

When I was a youngster playing American Legion ball, there wasn't a game that he and my mother weren't at. I played for the team in Newport. On the days we had practice, I'd hitchhike those 18 miles down I-67 and back.

But when we played our games on Sundays and Wednesdays, I knew I was riding to the game. That's because as sure as I was going to play shortstop, my parents were going to be in those stands rooting for me.

Sundays never posed a problem. We'd go to church in the morning and then all pile into an old car he had and drive to the game. If the game was at Newport, it was easy. If the game was at Batesville, about 40 miles from Swifton, it was a little tougher. But we always made it together.

Wednesdays were the problem. That was a work day for daddy. It didn't matter, though. Come three o'clock he would close the barber shop so that he could go to my game.

I never realized till many years later how much of a hardship that was on him. He needed the money bad to keep up with all the bills. Closing down the shop for three hours each week caused a hardship. He just figured nothing was more important than what mattered most to the family. He didn't care if he missed out on giving one haircut or a dozen of them. He was not going to miss a game for anything like that.

When I made it to the major leagues and we played in St. Louis against the old Browns, my mother and father would jump into that old car and drive up 250 miles for every series. Daddy would have to take days off of work again, but they were always there.

They didn't have the money to do that all the time, but that never mattered to them. I hope they realized how much that meant to me because I know I never would have made it without their support. I'm not ashamed to say I needed them. I'm not sure all parents realize how important that is to their children regardless of their age.

I played shortstop all the time I was growing up till I got moved over to third base after I signed with the Brooklyn Dodgers organization and their team at Newport. I enjoyed playing short-stop, but I just wasn't quick enough with my feet as a professional. I got moved to third and stayed there for the rest of my career.

I graduated from high school when I was just 16. Just after I turned 17 on August 23, I went to Arkansas State University in Jonesboro. I enrolled for the regular freshman courses.

It was extremely tough on my parents to send me to college. I had a National Youth Association scholarship, which paid a dollar a day for 15 days of work off campus. I worked in the kitchen for 30 cents an hour.

The problem was that room and board cost $15 a month, so that wiped out all of that money. Tuition and other expenses also cost $15 a month. Twice my daddy's checks bounced and I was called in about the payments. I never truly realized how much of a hardship it was on my parents to send me to college, but they felt it was important.

Arkansas State didn't have a baseball team, so I played on the intramural softball team. When I returned home in the spring, I started playing again with the Swifton Town Team.

I still had a dream to play major league baseball. My daddy shared that same dream with me. I was playing extremely well for the Town Team. We both were determined to keep chasing that dream as hard as we could and just see what happened.

My first break came the first spring out of college. Newport had a Class D team that was affiliated with the Brooklyn Dodgers. The postmaster in Swifton was Clyde Mitts. He was a rabid base-ball fan and used to drive down to watch almost all of the Newport home games.

After Newport lost a doubleheader one Sunday, he took it upon himself to talk to the general manager.

"We've got a boy in Swifton just 17 years old who can play shortstop better than anybody you have," Mr. Mitts told the general manager.

Everybody in Newport knew about me from playing American Legion baseball for four years.

"Well, if he's interested in playing, bring him on down here and we'll sign him to a contract," the general manager told him.

Mr. Mitts came straight to our house and talked to daddy and me.

"I want you to go to college first," daddy told me.

"Just let me try it and I'll go back to school afterward," I told him.

We talked for about an hour and I finally convinced him that playing baseball was the right thing for me. He told Mr. Mitts who immediately called the general manager.

"Have the boy here tomorrow and we'll sign him right after lunch," the general manager said. "Have that boy ready because he'll be in the lineup for tomorrow night's game."

Sure enough, I was in the starting lineup. A lot of people came down from Swifton because they knew I was going to play. I wasn't scared and I played all right at shortstop. But the first time up, I struck out on what must have been just three pitches.

I slammed my bat down so hard it bounced up in the air half-way down to third base. Before it hit the ground, I knew I had done wrong.

"You embarrassed us when you acted like that," daddy told me in the car on the drive home. "If you're going to play professional baseball, you're going to strike out and you're going to make mistakes. But always act like a professional. You've got the tools, but you also have to use your head."

I might have had some tools, but I did not find my first professional summer as easy as I did the sandlots. I played in about only 30 games that summer and batted .181.

I never felt overwhelmed or intimidated. I simply did not make that immediate adjustment to professional baseball. Around the first of August, they finally told me to go back home and make a fresh start in spring training.

They held spring training right down in Newport. When it did arrive, I was a completely different player. It was 1941 and I was 19 years old. I had gotten a little bigger and a little stronger. I lifted my batting average up from .181 that first pro season to .312. That was good for second in the league.

On March 24 of that year, I also celebrated one of the biggest days of my life. Hardly anybody knew about it then, but that was the day my first wife, Charlene, and I were secretly married.

Charlene and I had met back in the sixth grade. She came to our school from Alicia, about six miles up the road, after her daddy bought a farm a mile outside of Swifton. We started dating when we were only 14. It was never a matter of who Charlene or George were going to marry, only a question of when.

A friend of mine was the circuit clerk and I asked him what we needed to do to get married. He told me the license came out of his office and he could arrange for a justice of the peace. We wanted to be married at church so we went up to Hoxie and were married in the Methodist Church.

To this day, I have no idea why we wanted to keep our marriage a secret. Maybe both of us figured our parents wouldn't approve because of our age. After about two months, though, we decided that secrecy was silly. Charlene was visiting me on weekends in the rooming house I had in Newport. During the week, she was busy teaching school.

"I'm not surprised," my daddy said after I got up the nerve to tell him. "We knew it was going to happen, but you're both too young to be married. Now that you are, though, go out and make the best of it."

Suddenly, the world was mine. I was married to Charlene. I was playing baseball for a living. I jumped off to a quick start as soon as the season began. I played well in the field and hit all season long.

I was on my way. Nothing was going to stop me. At least that's what I thought.

CHAPTER FOUR

A TURN IN THE ROAD

Minor league baseball is something like going to a drive-in movie in the pouring rain. You get a chance to see the show, but you sometimes wonder if it's worth all the trouble.

The bus rides are brutal. You grab a meal whenever you can. Sometimes you eat only when you can afford it. The pay is horrible and a player really only exists on the dream that he may one day make the big leagues.

That's what kept me going. I was determined to make it to the top. After hitting .312 my first full year at Newport, I figured I was right on schedule.

At the end of the 1941 season, Newport sold my contract to Durham, which was a Class B club in the Dodger organization. So when the 1942 spring training was scheduled to start, they sent me a one-way train ticket from Swifton to Durham, North Carolina.

This was the first time I ever was going to play ball a pretty fair distance from Arkansas. I wasn't scared; I must admit, though, I realized then that professional baseball was going to demand a lot of sacrifices.

When I showed up in Durham, I was flat-out amazed at how many good players were there. The Dodgers were always known to have a wealth of good young players. Their farm system was massive, I found that out right quick. They must have had ten players competing for the third base job.

They only had a couple of shortstops, though, and toward the end of spring training, the Brooklyn Dodgers came to Durham to play a weekend exhibition series.

Bruno Betzold was the Durham manager. He asked if anyone could play shortstop. I already had been moved to third base, but I was determined to show the Dodgers that I could play with the big boys.

"I can play shortstop," I told him. "Just put me out there and let me show you what I can do."

All I cared about was getting a chance to play. I was able to come up with a half-dozen hits over the weekend. But I also made the same amount of errors. I wound up getting one of the biggest heartbreaks of my career when the Durham club flat-out released me.

There I was away from home for the first time, my wife was back in Swifton trying to make ends meet by teaching school, and I didn't even have enough money to buy a ticket to get on a train back to Arkansas. I called my mother, but all she could send me was $5. That wasn't even enough for a bus ticket.

It was right then that I came within a rabbit's hair of quitting baseball and taking a high-paying construction job for an army base they were building just outside of Durham.

Al Macli was a catcher from Brooklyn, New York. He had been released at the same time I was. He told me they were hiring workers for $7 an hour and encouraged me to join him.

That kind of pay was unheard of. When I had left Swifton, the same kind of work paid $1 an hour. I went with Al to fill out all the papers and was hired on the spot. When I returned to the hotel, Charlene already had left a message.

"You're a ball player," she said. "You're not going to work in a factory. We'll do whatever we have to do, but you are going to play baseball."

At the time, Charlene had more confidence in me than I did. I caught a break, though, because the Lancaster (Pennsylvania) team was coming to Durham for a series. Lancaster was affiliated with the Philadelphia Athletics, and according to Dodger scout Andy High, Lancaster needed a second baseman badly.

"You tell them I can play second base and I'll even clean up the clubhouse afterward," I told him.

I was willing to do anything to play. Andy got me a tryout with Lancaster and I wound up getting signed for $300 a month, which was more than I had made at Durham.

I felt like a little kid playing ball when I should have been in school. I played second base for six weeks before moving to third when Billy Long got drafted into the service. I finished the season with a .297 average and received a watch for being voted the team's Most Valuable Player.

I returned to Lancaster for the 1943 season. This time I brought along a lot more confidence. For the second straight season, I was voted MVP. Not only did I win another watch, but I also received a silver bat for leading all of minor league baseball with a .396 average. I played 120 games and finished with 221 hits.

Connie Mack was the owner of the Philadelphia Athletics. They had a working agreement with Lancaster, whereby in exchange for money, the Athletics would have their pick of any three players they wanted each year.

The regular minor league season ended just before Labor Day. It was the final Sunday of the season and we were getting ready for the playoffs. Word had spread that Mr. Mack was coming to watch our final game. Daddy was in town and finally said something about it to me before the game.

"No one wants to say anything to you because they don't want to get you nervous," he told me, "but the one player he is coming down to see is you. I thought you should know that."

I only hit five home runs that whole season. But one of them came on that Sunday. I also had a single and a double.

After the game, all the players were sitting around the clubhouse talking about the upcoming playoffs and just sort of celebrating the whole season. All of a sudden the room got so quiet I thought somebody had died. I looked up and saw Mr. Mack. It was just like God had walked into the room.

As he walked toward my locker, I remembered that daddy had said Mr. Mack was coming to see me.

"Mr. Kell, I'm Connie Mack," he said as he extended his hand to me. "How would you like to play in Philadelphia?"

I can't remember if I was sitting or standing at the time. When I heard his voice and shook his hand, I actually felt like I was floating in mid-air. He was wearing a necktie and that famous straw hat. This was the great Connie Mack. There was no owner bigger than him. In fact, I can't think of anybody in the game that he didn't overshadow in his own quiet and gentle way.

"Would I like to play in Philadelphia?" I repeated the question. "No more than I like Christmas and apple pie. Can I go with you right now?"

He told me to finish the playoffs with Lancaster. He then wanted me to play one game for the Athletics so that I would officially be part of the major league roster. The war was going on. He explained to me that if I were to be called into the service, I would receive credit for baseball pension time if I played at least one game.

Even though it seemed like an eternity, we won the playoffs. As soon as they were finished, I was on my way to Philadelphia. I was going to play in my first major league game!

Just before we left, Charlene had an idea that helped make things a little easier for us.

"Lancaster signed you for nothing and then got $20,000 for your contract," she reasoned. "I think you deserve a little something out of this."

I contacted the Lancaster general manager and expressed our concern.

"What would you like?" he asked.

At the time, we traveled to road games in three different cars. One of them was a 1937 DeSoto, which I drove.

"I'd like to have that DeSoto I drive and $500," I said.

He agreed so quickly that I probably could have asked for double the amount. But I was happy. It might have been the only game I would ever play in the major leagues. But I was on my way to Philadelphia.

We jumped into that DeSoto with just one thing on our minds. The next day, I was in the starting lineup at third base against the old St. Louis Browns.

I don't think there's any young player who ever forgets his first big league game. And if he's honest, I don't think there's any young player who won't tell you that his stomach starts to bubble like a pot of boiling water.

I was scared to death. I was more worried about making two or three errors than anything else. I was afraid I might mess up my whole career if I screwed up. After the first ball was hit to me, it was more or less like being at Lancaster and I settled down.

I walked out on that field before the game at Shibe Park and looked all around. I felt just like some kid in toyland. The Athletics didn't draw all that many people at the time, but there were far more than the 1,000 or 1,500 we drew in Lancaster.

I remember telling myself that even if I never played another major league game again in my life, at least I was there for one. I would be in the record books forever. I had made it.

Probably because I had hit .396 that year, the Browns were pulled around to left field on me my first time up. Their pitcher was a big left-hander named Al Milner.

I have no idea what kind of pitch I hit, but the first time up, I sliced a line drive over the first baseman's head. The ball curled down into the right field corner. By the time the ball got back into the infield, I was standing on third base with a triple.

I tried to act very calmly like it was just another time at bat for me. But I was dying to pinch myself to make sure this was all really happening.

When the game was over, Mr. Mack gave me a $100 bill and told me to go back home and be ready for spring training next March. We took off for Swifton in that DeSoto and never believed that anything in life could ever be better.

When we got home, I joined Charlene as a teacher in the junior high school. Because of the war, they were using anyone who had at least some college experience. I also coached the basketball team and studied as hard as the kids so that I wouldn't get shown up in class.

I can't explain exactly why I never was called into the service for the war. I had registered with the Selective Service at Newport. When I was getting ready to report to spring training with the Athletics, I reported to the agent that I would be in Philadelphia. I didn't want to be there for only a couple of weeks and then get a notice.

She made the records switch to Philadelphia, but I never received a call. I reported to camp the next spring training in 1944 with one whole major league game of experience under my belt.

I knew that the next time I had to leave Swifton, I was headed to the major leagues.

CHAPTER FIVE

"MY, MY" MR. MACK

A lot of people believe that Babe Ruth came along at a time in history and re-shaped the game of baseball. The game probably needed a giant like The Babe to restore its soul after the Black Sox scandal.

But if Babe Ruth re-shaped baseball, it was Mr. Connie Mack who gave the game its definition in the first place.

I've been so fortunate with all the good things that happened to me in baseball. Having been signed and having actually played for Mr. Mack is truly one of the real gifts with which I was blessed.

Sometimes we use the word "legend" too freely. We don't even think about the responsibilities that are attached to the term.

Connie Mack was, and still is, a true legend in American sports. There never was and never will be another character in baseball quite like Mr. Mack.

I never called him anything but "Mr. Mack." It was never "Connie" or "the manager" or "the owner." It was always "Mr. Mack." It didn't matter if I was talking directly to him or to someone else about him. It was always "Mr. Mack." I didn't do it because I had to. I did it because it was the right thing to do. It wasn't forced. It was natural.

That's the kind of person he was. He had such a presence about him. He carried himself with so much class and was so kind to everyone he met that it was impossible to think about calling him anything other than "Mr. Mack."

You didn't wonder if Mr. Mack was around. You didn't have to see him. You could just feel his presence.

Mr. Mack was such a special person. It's absolutely safe to say that nobody will ever come close to touching the records he set in his career. That's impossible.

Mr. Mack managed for 53 years! He won 3,731 games. I don't care how good a manager anyone else might be, there's no way anyone is going to even get close. Until the Yankees came along with their dynasty, nobody won as many pennants and World Series as Mr. Mack's teams had.

It was different, of course, because Mr. Mack also owned the Athletics and wasn't about to fire himself as the manager. Still, what he did for baseball with all of his accomplishments and his ideals, the game will never be able to repay him.

It wasn't just all of the records that he set that made him so special. He was such a good man and he was so kind. I don't know of an enemy that he ever had. I don't know of a player who played for him that didn't admire and respect him.

He always looked just like all those old pictures you see of him. He never wore a uniform; he was always dressed neatly in a dark suit with a white shirt that had a high starched collar and a necktie. He always carried around a scorecard. Whenever he wanted to talk to someone, he'd motion them over with that scorecard.

He always had time to talk to everybody. It didn't matter if you were one of his star players or a member of the grounds crew. If you had something to say to Mr. Mack, he had the time to listen.

When you played for Mr. Mack, you never received meal money on the road. A player would simply sign the tab and Mr. Mack would take care of it. He trusted his boys.

That policy didn't change until one year late in Mr. Mack's career when one of our pitchers got knocked out of the game in about the third inning. He went back to the restaurant in the hotel early and ordered himself a big meal and who knows how many bottles of champagne. The bill totaled out at about $100. After that, we were gently reminded to use discretion.

After meals on the road I used to love to sit in the lobby and just listen to the stories Mr. Mack would spin. He'd sit there in a big chair and talk about all the good times with his championship teams in 1928-29-30 and 31. He had guys like Al Simmons and Jimmy Dykes and Lefty Grove. I sat there for hours listening to the same stories all the time and loved it. I felt like I was listening to Moses.

By the time I got to the Athletics, Mr. Mack was 80 years old. So he wasn't a good manager by then, and I didn't expect him to be. We didn't have a whole lot of talent at that time so there really wasn't that much strategy he could have used anyway. Al Simmons was one of his coaches and Mr. Mack relied on him quite a bit.

Our starting pitcher went nine innings unless he was getting his head hammered. We had one guy who would pinch hit for the pitcher and one guy who was used as a pinch runner. Mr. Mack kept both of them on the bench till the eighth or ninth inning so that if it was a close game, he could use them.

There was a game in Philadelphia when we were one run down in the ninth. Our leadoff man singled and Mr. Mack sent Jo Jo White in to run for him. Simmons was coaching third base. Before White got in the game, Simmons stopped him. He walked over to the dugout to talk to Mr. Mack.

"Mr. Mack, you may need a pinch hitter in just a minute and Jo Jo is our best man," Simmons said. "You can send anybody out there to run."

"My, my," Mr. Mack said. "I hadn't thought about that."

So he sent another player out to pinch run.

"My, my" was about the strongest epithet that ever came out of Mr. Mack's mouth. He never used profanity.

There was a time he took out one of our pitchers who was getting his brains beat out. When that pitcher got back to the dugout, he directed a profanity toward Mr. Mack. The dugout suddenly became as quiet as a church. Mr. Mack slowly started to walk toward the pitcher. We all wondered just what he was going to say.

"Well, horsefeathers to you, too, sir," Mr. Mack said and calmly walked back to his usual spot in the dugout.

Our lineup was the same almost every day. Mr. Mack used to write it out in long hand and give it to the umpire before the game. I used to bat fifth in the lineup and Irv Hall, our second baseman, usually followed me.

We were playing the White Sox one day and the first time up, I singled. Jimmy Dykes was managing Chicago at the time. After one pitch to Hall, Dykes walked up to home plate umpire Cal Hubbard.

"That man on first base is supposed to be batting now," Dykes said.

Mr. Mack didn't exactly have perfect penmanship. He had accidentally scribbled H-A-L-L into the fifth spot instead of K-E-L-L.

"That's the way they always bat," Mr. Mack said.

"Well, you've got to write it that way, Mr. Mack," Hubbard said. "We can't read your mind."

So I was called out after getting a base hit.

"My, my," was Mr. Mack's response.

Even if his managerial skills had slipped, Mr. Mack never changed as a person. He was so sincere, and his word was his bond.

His son, Earl, coached first base. Toward the end of the 1945 season, Earl called me over before the start of a game.

"George, daddy really likes you," Earl said. "He likes the way you hustle all the time. You give him your best every day and we all think you are going to get nothing but better. He said he wants to give you a thousand dollar bonus at the end of the season."

One thousand dollars was a lot of money in those days. Charlene about fell out of her chair when I told her.

Once the season ended, no one said anything to me about the bonus. I stayed in Philadelphia waiting for a call. I felt strange, but finally I called Mr. Mack and asked if I could visit him. He told me to come to his office in the tower of Shibe Park.

"Mr. Mack, this is out of character for me," I started, "but it also means a lot to me. Earl said that you had told him that you were going to give me a thousand dollar bonus at the end of the season."

Mr. Mack seemed unaware of the situation and I thought that maybe it wasn't true. He called Earl to his office.

"Did we promise this young man a thousand dollar bonus?" Mr. Mack asked his son.

"Yes, daddy," Earl answered. "You said you like the way he plays the game and always bears down and hustles."

Mr. Mack immediately called in his secretary and had a check made out to me. At his age, it had sort of slipped his mind. But once he discovered he had made a promise, he was going to keep it.

A few years after I had been traded to Detroit, the Tigers had my brother, Skeeter, up at the park for a tryout. He was a second baseman and worked out for a few days. Red Rolfe was the manager and I asked him if the Tigers were going to sign him.

"I don't think he's going to make it," Rolfe said.

Philadelphia happened to be in town for a series. Before one of the games, Mr. Mack motioned me over to his dugout with his scorecard.

"Is that your brother working out over there, Mr. Kell?" he asked.

"Yes sir, it is," I answered.

"Are the Tigers going to sign him?" he asked.

"No sir, I don't think they're interested," I said. "My daddy wants him to go to college and all he wants for a bonus is scholarship money."

"Then you tell him to come see me," Mr. Mack said. "I signed one Kell and I'm darn sure I'd like to have another one."

Mr. Mack gave Skeeter the money to go to Arkansas State and he wound up graduating. Skeeter also made it to the Athletics for one season before he retired from the game.

I've got to be one of the few men left who ever played for Mr. Connie Mack. Over its history, baseball has had its share of characters that have molded the game. I've been lucky to have met a lot of them.

None were anything like Mr. Connie Mack. I am so proud I had the opportunity to play for him.

CHAPTER SIX
THE WAR YEARS

My first two years in the big leagues came during strange times in our history. Strange for baseball and strange for the country.

The world was at war. It changed the course of our national history. It also left an indelible mark on baseball that will last forever.

So many players were called into military service. Some of that era's brightest young prospects never got the chance to see their baseball careers grow. Many of the game's big-name stars had their careers interrupted. Who knows how many records might have been set without this bloody disruption that overshadowed all American enterprises?

It was difficult for me to accurately measure the war's impact on my own career. This was the first time I had reached the major leagues. I couldn't identify a precise difference because I had no first-hand experience to compare it to.

There were ball players who played during the war who had been in the major leagues for several years. They had been fringe players for maybe seven or eight years. Suddenly they became regulars because a lot of the stars were gone.

So it's tough for me to say if I felt any different at that time. It was my first taste of the big leagues. I really didn't know. But I could sense something.

All I remember is being worried about my brother, Frank, who was in the Air Force. I prayed for his safety every day. I worried a lot about what was going on in the world. Like everyone else, I couldn't understand why the whole world had to be at war.

Judge (Kenesaw Mountain) Landis was the Baseball Commissioner at the time. He offered to shut down major league baseball until the war was over. President Roosevelt appreciated the offer but refused.

He said something like, "Baseball is good for the country. We've got so many good Americans putting in so much time in the factories to support our war efforts and they've got to have some recreation. For some, going to ball games is the only recreation they have. I want major league baseball to continue."

But the war definitely took its toll on the quality of play throughout the major leagues. Sometimes it was subtle. There just wasn't that crispness or that edge that you expect to see in the big leagues. You could see it in every position on the field. I think it was most apparent in the pitching. Some players who might never really have had a chance at the major leagues got a shot at a dream they never thought they'd have.

I really noticed the difference in 1946 when the war was over. All the big boys were back. Guys like (Ted) Williams and (Joe) DiMaggio and a whole long list returned to take their regular spots. Like all other segments of our society, baseball fulfilled its duty. Now that the boys were back, we'd all see what we were missing.

I remember telling myself that I was fortunate to have played two years before these guys came back. I knew that guys like Williams and DiMaggio were a lot better than me. With those two years under my belt, though, I felt like I could at least hold my own.

I was actually fortunate to break into the big leagues at that time. I was making a jump all the way from Class B ball to the major leagues. I was getting on-the-spot training against the big boys. Or at least all of the big boys who hadn't been called into the service.

Even going to my first big league spring training in 1944 was different than most. Because of the war, instead of training in Florida, teams were training closer to home because of travel restrictions.

We trained in Frederick, Maryland, which is only about 150 miles south of Philadelphia, so it wasn't much warmer. For exhibition games, we played a lot of the service teams that were based around Washington, D.C. The interesting part is that those teams had a lot of major leaguers playing for them. It made for some pretty good exhibition games.

I showed up at spring training just dumb enough to think that I was going to be the regular third baseman. I looked around at all the players and couldn't see anybody taking the job away from me.

On the very first day I took batting and infield practice with the first team. I played every exhibition game and took it for granted that third base belonged to me. Mr. Mack put me in the lineup, turned it over to me, and that's where I stayed.

Just being in the big leagues made every day special. Here I was—a little boy from Swifton, Arkansas—traveling with the Philadelphia Athletics into some of the biggest cities in the United States.

There was a feeling of awe going to cities like New York, Detroit, Boston and Chicago. I took some comfort in the fact that I was traveling with 24 other guys who were basically in the same boat I was. Most of them had come from small cities so at least I had company.

When I got to New York for the first time, it was overwhelming. I walked down those streets staring straight up. I couldn't believe all those buildings. There were more skyscrapers in New York than there were people in Swifton. Who were all those people and how could all of them fit into one city? There must have been more people on one block than there were in the whole town back home.

Nothing compared to my first trip to Yankee Stadium. I went out there real early before my first game. I must have walked every inch of that park, on the field and off. I couldn't believe I was actually walking over the same field that Babe Ruth and Lou Gehrig and all those great Yankees had played on. I looked up at that triple deck and couldn't imagine that 70,000 people could show up for a game here.

In those days the Yankees used the third base dugout. There was a foul pop fly that I chased down all the way into the Yankee dugout to end a game. I took one step down, stuck up my glove and squeezed that ball like my life depended on it. A group of Yankees sort of gathered together to make sure I didn't fall.

Before the game the next day, Charlie Keller told me that Joe McCarthy (Yankee manager) said, "that Kell kid is going to be a real ball player...that kid is going to make it."

There I was in Yankee Stadium and the great Joe McCarthy told one of his players that "I was going to make it."

I felt like a millionaire. I didn't know what I was going to do... I didn't know how I was going to do it ... but I promised myself that I was going to make it. Joe McCarthy had said so.

We traveled by train in those days. I enjoyed it, but I much prefer the airplane travel of today. A lot of people say that train travel promoted more team camaraderie. I believe camaraderie is overplayed. You can get all the camaraderie you want in the clubhouse and out on the field before a game.

Traveling by plane gets a player some extra time to spend with his family. Of course, back when I played, the longest trip was to St. Louis, which is just a minor hop nowadays.

We'd each get our own little compartment on the train. Some of the guys used to play cards. I'd pull down my bed and either read a book or just stare at all the fields and little towns we passed. A lot of them reminded me of Swifton. I had to remind myself that I was headed for the next big city as a member of the Philadelphia Athletics.

I've always been an avid reader. Ever since I was a kid right through today, there's nothing I find more interesting than a good book. Primarily I read history and biographies. I love reading about politics. My favorites are books on world history and the war—why did we get into World War II...what made Hitler who he was.

I have a whole library of hardcover books at home in Swifton. Inside each one of the covers I've written a little note. I'd write what day I bought the book and where it was purchased. Then I'd include a few sentences on what happened in our game the previous night.

My oldest grandson is 26 years old. He loves to come over to the house and thumb through all the books and read where his granddaddy bought them. He enjoys my little descriptions of the games and trying to get a feel on how the team was doing at the time.

I wasn't a loner. I just enjoyed going to dinner after a game and then going up to my room and getting into a good book. I didn't drink alcohol. I was 30 years old and had been in the major leagues for quite a while before I drank my first glass of beer. I don't even recall the occasion for having it.

I felt comfortable those first two years in Philadelphia even though it was a time of adjustment both on and off the field. Hitting had always come pretty natural to me. Back in Swifton, I was a kid hitting off of grown men. I never had any trouble. Once I got to Newport and then Lancaster, I just kept hitting the same way I had all my life.

When I finally made it to the majors, though, hitting didn't come all that easy right off the reel. Even during those war years, pitchers up in the big leagues worked the hitters differently. They didn't wind up and just try to blow the ball by you. They knew how to set a hitter up. They had an idea of how they were going to pitch each hitter before the batter even came up to the plate.

The year before my rookie season with Philadelphia, I had led all the minor leagues with a .396 average. But when I made it with the Athletics, I was in way over my head.

I went from Class B to the major leagues. I no longer could just go over to the bat rack, pick up a bat and walk up there and get a hit without hardly thinking about it. I had to refine my whole approach to hitting. I had to work very hard at it.

Not to make any excuses, but I had three or four coaches giving me tips on what to do and what not to do. They were just trying to help, but I was getting so much advice that my head couldn't get the message to my hands quick enough to handle a fastball or tangle with a curve. At least not the right message.

Finally, one day before a game, Mr. Mack called his coaches together.

"Leave the young man alone," Mr. Mack told them. "He's hit wherever he's been. He's either led the league or finished second in every league he's played in. Don't worry, he'll hit."

I struggled that first year and hit .268 in 139 games. The next year I batted .272 in 147 games. I was getting a chance to play and the opportunity to become a better player. I took that opportunity to work as hard as I could to repay the confidence that Mr. Mack had shown in me.

Al Simmons was one of our coaches and he did give me a good piece of advice that I carried throughout my career. Simmons was a strong figure who wound up being elected into the Hall of Fame in 1953. He knew hitting. He understood all of the little nuances that separate an average hitter from a good one. He also appreciated a player who was willing to sweat and bleed in order to improve.

Simmons told me I had been standing too far away from the plate in the batter's box. That made me hit too many balls to right field. He told me that if I moved up right on top of the plate, I'd become a much more aggressive hitter and be able to use all parts of the field.

"The pitchers up here see what you're doing," he told me. "When you're way back in that box, they're going to keep pitching you away and you're going to keep poking the ball to right.

"Now if you move up closer to the plate, you're going to be able to pull that ball to left and still go to right on an outside pitch. You might get hit right between the eyes one day if you're not careful. But this will keep you much more alert."

I moved way up in the box and got so close to the plate my toes were practically touching it. I dared a pitcher to pitch me inside. I'd turn on it and line it to left. If he pitched me away, I'd go with the pitch to right. That made me a good hit-and-run batter and a good two-strike hitter. I never struck out much because I could move the ball to any field I had to.

I worked hard on each part of my hitting during batting practice every day. The biggest fault with a lot of hitters today begins right with batting practice. Instead of trying to refine their swings, they try to hit every ball over the roof.

I started batting practice by going up the middle. Then I'd concentrate on moving the ball to right. My last few swings I worked on pulling the ball and maybe hitting with a little more power.

Hitting is just like any other discipline in life. A great pianist doesn't simply show up at a concert and start banging on the piano. By the time he arrives, he's practiced every number so many times the tips of his fingers are callused.

Once the war was over and all of the big boys were back, the caliber of play was definitely turned up. I was happy to have had a couple of years to prepare for their return.

In 1946, we opened the season in Philadelphia against the Yankees. The night before the opener, I remember lying in bed as nervous as I ever was in the big leagues.

Being nervous on a baseball field is not as bad as a lot of people think. I believe you play a little better if you know how to harness that nervous energy properly. I know there were three or four hard hit balls right at me. After handling them, I knew I would be all right.

I was nervous because when the Yankees showed up this time, they were bringing all their weapons. The war was over and all the boys were back. There was Joe DiMaggio. There was Charlie Keller. And there was Bill Dickey behind the plate. All the stars were back. Now we'd find out what the big leagues were really all about, I told myself the night before that opener.

When I went to bat for the first time, Dickey introduced himself to me. Dickey is from Little Rock, Arkansas, and he had been one of my idols my whole life.

"Don't worry, kid," he told me. "You've been here a couple of years now. You're going to be a good ball player. Everything's going to be all right."

I'll always remember that moment. The thought of Bill Dickey encouraging me was really something special. It helped me through a lot of tough times.

The toughest part of that era for me actually occurred after the war in 1946. I already had been traded to Detroit when our family received word that my brother, Frank, had been killed in Germany while serving in the army of occupation.

The war had been over. Frank had survived. Then he and a fellow pilot were killed by what may have been an act of sabotage. My whole family had trouble reconciling the fact that Frank had survived the war only to die when it was over.

I was the last one in our family to see Frank. It was in September when the Tigers were playing a series in Philadelphia and we stayed at the Warwick Hotel. Frank and another boy were stationed at Fort Dix. They came up to spend the weekend before being shipped to Germany as part of the army of occupation.

We had a great time and really felt quite relieved that the war was finally over. Three months later and the hell my parents prayed they would escape struck home.

In December, my parents received a telegram that said Frank was seriously ill and that the Air Force would keep them informed. As it turned out, my parents were not kept informed.

The next communication did not come until February. This time the telegram said that Frank had actually died in December. The telegram also said that the Air Force was going to bury him in Germany. That was something my father would not allow to happen no matter what he had to do.

My father contacted Congressman Wilbur Mills who was chairman of the Ways and Means Committee and a very powerful man in Washington. The very next day, Mr. Mills called my father to tell him that Frank's body would be shipped back to the United States immediately. We buried Frank in the Swifton Cemetery next to his wife's brother.

My father was not one to show much emotion. He kept everything inside. My mother fell to pieces. We had to keep her sedated for almost a month.

Frank and a fellow pilot were the victims of what may have been sabotage. After returning from a flying mission they died of asphyxiation from a gas stove that had been booby-trapped.

About ten years later, I visited Frankfort during a goodwill mission for the Air Force to conduct some baseball clinics. I did all the research I could to find the house where my brother had died but I wasn't successful.

Frank was a pretty good ball player himself. If he hadn't enlisted into the service, my father may have realized his dream of having all three of his boys play in the major leagues.

Instead, Frank sacrificed his life for his country. It's the worst memory from those war time years that anyone in the Kell family has had to endure.

CHAPTER SEVEN

HELLO DETROIT

P layer trades in baseball are as much a part of the game as the seventh-inning stretch. They're great for the fans. They spike interest in the game. Hopefully, a trade is good for each team and both clubs finish a little higher in the standings because of the deal.

About the only ones who really feel funny about a trade are the players themselves. At least that's the way I felt the first time I was traded.

As things worked out, getting traded to Detroit was the best thing that ever happened to my career. When you're a 23-year-old youngster still trying to establish yourself in the major leagues, though, getting traded is like trying to solve a jigsaw puzzle with one piece missing.

I was stunned. I tried to put all the pieces together real quickly in my mind. I felt like an orphan; I felt like nobody in the world wanted me to play baseball for them.

Obviously, ever since I was a little kid and followed major league baseball, I knew that players were traded. As a matter of fact, I enjoyed reading about all those trades and trying to figure out which team got the better end of the deal.

When I was playing for Philadelphia, though, it just never occurred to me that players were actually traded. I was playing every day. I hustled and I was batting .299 at the time. I knew that Mr. Mack liked me, so getting traded was probably the furthest thing from my mind.

So why did it happen? The first thing that went through my mind was that nobody wanted me. They had to do something, so they got rid of me.

It wasn't until everything settled and I was able to sort out a few things in my mind that I began to feel more comfortable. Somebody must have wanted me. If the Tigers were willing to trade Barney McCosky for me, evidently they wanted me pretty badly.

Before he got called into the military service for the war, McCosky never hit lower than .293 in four seasons for the Tigers. Plus, he was a hometown boy who had made it to the big leagues. He had played in a World Series for the Tigers.

McCosky had established himself as a legitimate star. I couldn't understand why the Tigers would trade somebody like him for an unknown third baseman. That's what I felt like in the deal—the unknown third baseman.

I guess the Tigers didn't have anybody at the position coming up in their system. Evidently, they thought a young player like me might work out for the future.

I'll never forget the date. It was May 18, 1946. And the funny thing about it is that the Athletics were in Detroit finishing a series at the time.

In those days, like most teams, the Athletics took trains on all their road trips. We had a chance to fly a charter out of Detroit to St. Louis for our next stop. The players were given the option of flying or traveling by train. I already had voted to take the plane.

I had just finished eating breakfast in the old Book-Cadillac Hotel and was getting on the elevator to go back to my room. I was going to pack up my belongings and head to the park for the last game of the series.

As I was getting onto the elevator, Mr. Mack arrived.

"George, I need to talk to you," Mr. Mack said.

"All right, Mr. Mack," I answered. "I'm going upstairs to pack my suitcase. As soon as I get to the park, I'll come to your office."

"No," Mr. Mack responded. "I need to talk to you right now. Please follow me to my suite."

I was somewhat surprised at why we had to meet before we went to the park. After I found out, I was totally shocked.

"You're going to stay here, George," Mr. Mack told me.

I thought he believed I didn't want to fly to St. Louis.

"No, Mr. Mack," I said. "I already voted to fly, so I'll be going with the team right after the game."

Mr. Mack got real serious, but he gave it to me straight.

"No, George," he said. "I traded you to Detroit."

I suppose I just sort of sat there and then said something like, "Oh, you traded me...I stay here."

Then it hit me like a line drive to the nose. I no longer played for Mr. Mack. I no longer had the same teammates I had for the last two years. I no longer was a member of the Philadelphia Athletics.

"Yes, I traded you," he repeated. "I didn't want to trade you, George. But you are going to be a very good ball player and you are going to make a lot of money. You will be much better off playing for Detroit. I can't afford to pay the kind of money you have a chance to make. This is a tremendous opportunity for you."

Of course, I listened to everything Mr. Mack had to say. At the time, though, the words sort of bounced around in my head like a bad-hop grounder. I thought that this was the type of thing that baseball executives told all the players who were traded.

It wasn't until later that I understood everything that Mr. Mack had told me was true. He was being honest. He was sincere about everything he had told me. That's the kind of man he was.

I went over to the visitors clubhouse at Briggs Stadium (what the park was called at the time) to pick up my glove and spikes. While I was clearing out my locker, McCosky arrived.

There were writers and photographers all around McCosky. He was a hometown hero and this was a much bigger deal in Detroit than it was in Philadelphia. I felt like Cinderella being traded for the queen of the ball. Barney and I posed for pictures together before I walked over to the other clubhouse. My new clubhouse.

"Does this bother you being traded to Detroit?" I remember McCosky asked me.

"I never did expect it, but Mr. Mack explained to me that I would have a brighter future in Detroit," I answered.

I remember McCosky looking at me. I know he didn't want to leave Detroit. He probably felt a whole lot worse than I did. But he was a veteran. He must have sensed how displaced I was feeling.

"You'll be better off in Detroit," he said. "You're going to love it here. I hate to leave because this is home. I've had good years here. I went to school here. My family is here."

Suddenly it dawned on me that my family was in Philadelphia. George, Jr. had been born on September 6, 1945, about seven months before I was traded. Charlene, the baby and I had been living in a hotel there. When we couldn't afford to stay in the hotel anymore, we moved into an old row house. I had gotten to know this old Italian gentleman who used to go to Shibe Park every day. He lived alone and invited us to rent his place. He moved down into the basement. We had been there only about ten days when I got traded.

I called Charlene to tell her what had happened. Needless to say, she was just as shocked as I was. She didn't know what to do. We decided it would be best for her and George, Jr. to return to Swifton until things settled. There was one major problem—she didn't have enough money to make the trip.

After the game, I called my parents and asked if my brother, Skeeter, could drive Charlene and the baby home. Daddy bought Skeeter a Greyhound Bus ticket to Philadelphia. Charlene and Skeeter packed up the old DeSoto and drove home to Swifton.

Mr. Mack had instructed me to report to George Trautman as soon as I arrived at the ball park. He was the general manager and his office was on the third floor.

He told me how much the Tigers wanted me in Detroit. He told me this was the perfect place for a good young player to establish his career. Then he asked how much money I was making.

I told him that the first year I played in Philadelphia I made $3,000. I made $5,000 the second. The previous winter Mr. Mack had sent me a contract for $6,500. I'll never know how I drummed up the nerve to question Mr. Mack, but I told him that I played every day and a .272 average for a third baseman wasn't all that bad. He said that he agreed and "there was nothing that we couldn't work out."

Mr. Mack told me that if I kept hustling and improving like I had, he'd give me an extra $2,000 at the end of the 1946 season. I trusted Mr. Mack and told him his word was as good as gold with me.

"You've already hustled and improved more than you realize," Trautman told me. "If you weren't a good player already, I wouldn't have traded for you."

He called in his secretary, Alice Sloane, and had her type up a contract for $8,500.

"Now go out and play ball the way we know you can and we'll take care of you at the end of the season," he said.

And he did. I hit .327 for the Tigers. On the last day of the season before the game, Trautman called me up to his office.

"You earned your $8,500," he said. "And then some. We want to sign you right now for next year at $11,500. Plus we're going to give you a $2,500 bonus."

I was floored. I had to pretend I knew this was how business was conducted all the time. I must have reached for that pen like I was trying to grab a line drive.

That was a total of $14,000! I felt right then and there that I was going home to Swifton as the richest man in town.

Mr. Mack had been right. Detroit was the ideal spot for me to play ball. In fact, there weren't too many players in the league who didn't want to come to Detroit. I believe Detroit and Boston were the two finest cities where a young man could really develop into a good player if he showed determination.

For a hitter, Briggs Stadium and Fenway Park were the closest things to heaven that any player could imagine. Both ball parks are paradise for hitters. The background is perfect. The field conditions were always ideal. And the fans know their baseball better than anywhere else in the country.

Detroit fans have always been so loyal and fun to play for. Detroiters, especially back then, were primarily blue-collar people. They are honest and work hard for a living. When they want to relax, they go out to the ball park or a football game.

Because of their own work ethic, they recognize when a player is giving everything he has or is just going through the motions. That's the way it should be. Those fans have a right to demand the best when they spend their hard-earned money at the ball park. I've never had a problem with fans wanting the most for their dollar.

One of the reasons I felt so comfortable in Detroit was that I always had quite a few fans from Arkansas pulling for me from the stands. After the war, when the automobile factories returned to regular production, there was a considerable migration of the work force from the south up to Detroit.

I think at one point, half of Jackson County, where Swifton is located, had moved up north to work in the factories. I knew so many people and they really made me feel at home.

I needed all the help I could get. I didn't let the pressure get to me, but I knew it was there. Being traded for a hometown hero like Barney McCosky isn't exactly the best first step in establishing a relationship with a city. It was not a very popular trade with the fans and I knew it the first day I put on that uniform with the old English "D."

I felt there were a lot of people who wondered if the Tigers knew what they were doing trading one of their favorite players for some third baseman they hadn't even heard of.

Two things helped to pull the fans into my corner. H.G. Salsinger worked for *The Detroit News* and was the most powerful sportswriter in town. He wrote a story telling the fans to relax about the McCosky-for-Kell trade. He figured that the Tigers had picked me up just in time. His sources told him that the Red Sox had been on the verge of getting me just before the Tigers completed the deal. With the exception of Ted Williams, the Red Sox had given Mr. Mack his pick of any of their outfielders for me. And they had a pretty impressive list of outfielders at the time. After that story appeared, the fans began to view me with a little more appreciation.

Even more important than that story, though, was the season I put together. Right off the reel I started hitting and never cooled down all year long.

Steve O'Neill was the manager and he was such a gracious man. He made me feel that the Tigers couldn't have moved up in the standings if they had not made the deal for me. One day he told somebody that, "Kell is the best third baseman since Buck Weaver played the position." I didn't even know who Buck Weaver was. Coming from O'Neill, though, it sounded like a compliment and I was proud.

I kept my batting average up around .320 all year long. Toward the end of the season, I wanted to finish above .300 more than anything in the world. I had always done it in the minor leagues and it felt so easy. Now I had a chance to do it with the Tigers and I didn't want to blow the opportunity.

With about ten days left to play in the season, I was batting .315. We were playing in Cleveland and I had a 6-for-6 day that pushed me up to .324.

I knew right then I had a .300 season in my back pocket. I could cruise in the rest of the way. The fans already had taken a liking to me. I also played well in the field and made only five errors all year.

Life couldn't have been better for me than in Detroit. It was an excellent place to play ball. The fans were great. They were honest and enthusiastic. And the city was a beautiful place in which to live.

Most of the years I played in Detroit we lived on the northwest side of the city on Oakfield. We rented the home from Steve Gromek who pitched for the Cleveland Indians. It cost me $750 rent for the whole season and it was in one of the prettiest neighborhoods you'd ever want to live in.

In those days, Detroit had a population of more than one-and-a-half million. Most of them were working-class people and everybody was proud of their homes and kept up the neighborhoods.

If a player played in the National League in those days he most likely wanted to play for the Dodgers or the Cardinals. American League players always preferred the Tigers and the Red Sox.

Every time I would see Mr. Mack after that I would thank him for what he had done for my career.

There was a time when I wouldn't have dared to dream of playing anywhere but in Philadelphia. After getting an opportunity to play in Detroit, however, I knew the deal was a break for my career.

Mr. Mack had done me a favor. Now the rest was up to me.

CHAPTER EIGHT

THE PERFECT PLACE TO BE

There wasn't a day I didn't enjoy playing in Detroit. As soon as I got over the nervousness from being traded for Barney McCosky, I felt I had the chance to get better and better.

Detroit was the perfect place for me to play. It's always been a great sports town. The fans there know their sports and appreciate players who perform like they want to be there.

Detroit is a big city without all the hassles of New York or the frills of Chicago or some other major cities. It was easy for me to identify with all the Detroit fans. I think they appreciated my work ethic. I may have gone hitless or made an error in a game, but I never cheated them out of their money.

The crowds were always so big and enthusiastic in Detroit. I was there when they put in lights for the first night game; the people were standing in the aisles. It was almost like a World Series game. As a player, I loved every minute of it.

I wasn't quite convinced how good I might become. I had a feeling, though, that Detroit was where I belonged. I felt good with the Tigers because I knew that they really wanted me. I felt comfortable living in the community because all of the fans made me feel at home.

Mr. Walter O. Briggs owned the Tigers at the time. He was different, of course, from Mr. Mack. Mr. Mack not only owned the Athletics, he served as manager. He also was pretty much his own general manager, scouting director and just about everything else he needed to make the franchise go.

Mr. Briggs was what was called in those days a "sportsman." He had been highly successful in the manufacturing industry and was fairly well off financially. He had a love affair for baseball and the Tigers became the passion of his life.

He was a good man to play for because he was the classic owner of that period. He loved to watch his boys play. He came out to the park for a lot of the games. But he never interfered with the manager or the operation of the team. He never hung around the clubhouse trying to become "one of the boys."

Everybody knew who Mr. Briggs was. But the players had very little contact with him.

At the beginning of each season, one of his attendants would bring him into the clubhouse in his wheelchair. Mr. Briggs would go around the whole room to shake hands with all the players and coaches. All he wanted to do was to wish everybody good luck.

He did the same thing at the end of the season. He wanted to thank everybody for trying to play as hard as they could all year. He always wanted the fans to get their money's worth.

The closest personal contact I had with him came between games of a doubleheader we were playing in Detroit.

I don't recall what we had done in the first game, but my uniform had gotten dirty. I was a pretty hard-nosed player, so I always was getting dirt and grass stains on my pants and jersey from diving for a ball or sliding into a base.

We were loosening up for the second game. We were tossing baseballs just outside our dugout. In the stands from the side of the dugout, I heard somebody calling my name. Mr. Briggs' attendant had wheeled him right down to the rail.

"Mr. Kell," the attendant called. "Mr. Briggs would like to have a brief word with you."

I fired that baseball to the player I was playing catch with and hustled over to the rail.

"George," he said quietly and very politely. "Don't you have a clean uniform to put on for the second game?"

I quickly glanced down at my jersey and my pants and noticed the usual grime I generally accumulated during a game. I used to concentrate so much on what I was doing that I never really paid attention to how my uniform looked.

"Yes sir," I said somewhat meekly.

He sort of broke a little smile and then nodded his head toward the clubhouse.

"I'd rather you go put it on," he said. "You've got enough time. And you'd look so much better."

I hustled off that field as fast as I tried to leg out an extra base hit. I switched into a fresh jersey and a clean pair of pants and came running out as fast as I had dashed in there.

When I got back to the field, Mr. Briggs already had left for his usual location to watch the second game. When I spotted him in the stands he already had noticed me back on the field. He had that little smile and didn't say anything else.

He was polite. He didn't mean to cause any problem. He simply felt that big league players should look like big leaguers. The fans had a right to expect that.

Soon after I announced my retirement from broadcasting, I received a letter from one of Mr. Briggs' daughters. I saved every note I received, but I put this one in an especially safe spot.

In the letter she said, "You were my daddy's favorite ball player and I admire you so much." I couldn't believe after all those years that she would take the time to remember me like that. That truly meant a lot to me.

Hitting over .300 my first year in Detroit was one of the greatest accomplishments of my career. In my mind, I felt I had earned the confidence the Tigers had shown by trading for me. I also proved to myself and the rest of the league that I was a .300 hitter...even after all the big boys had come home from the war.

Steve O'Neill was the manager. He penciled me in the lineup the first day I got there and that's where I stayed. Except for about a two-and-a-half-week period where I was out with a pulled muscle in my leg, I played every day.

Right off the reel, I jumped to a fast start for the Tigers in 1946. I was hitting well and playing third base like I had been there all my life. I didn't think anything could stop me until later in the season when I pulled that muscle. I couldn't believe it. It was the first time in my life I had ever been hurt.

I was sitting on the bench for about a week. My mind was hurting more than my leg, because I wanted to get back into that lineup more than anything in the world. During the games I used to walk up and down that bench in the dugout. I kept pleading with O'Neill to put me back into the lineup.

"This kind of injury takes time to heal," he told me. "A pulled muscle is serious. You need rest and a lot of whirlpools."

I think he finally got tired of me badgering him to get back into the lineup. Against his better judgment, he penciled me in.

After I returned, the first time up I sent a line shot into the corner down the left field line. I must have drilled that ball because I had to run as hard as I could and slide into second for a two-base hit.

Suddenly the pain struck like a knife. I couldn't stand up. I had pulled that same muscle again. I couldn't walk even if a brand new contract was riding on the line. I was out for another week-and-a-half and O'Neill wasn't smiling about it.

"From now on, I'll decide when you go back in the lineup," he told me.

In spite of that injury, I worked hard and had a terrific season. Throughout my whole life, at every level I played, I was honest enough with myself to realize there were a number of players with a whole lot more talent than I had.

I made up the difference by desire. I had a dream to make it to the major leagues and I made it. I wanted to make myself a .300 hitter and a solid all-around player and I did that, too. There were players who worked as hard as I did. But I promised myself when I was just a boy that nobody would work any harder than I did.

When I was a youngster back home in Swifton, there was another young boy who signed with Newport in the Class D League with me. He was a catcher who could hit with power. There really was no doubt that he had more physical tools than I did.

He came off a farm out in the country and had spent his whole young life farming with his daddy. When he was moved up to Durham, he quit playing baseball. He just did not have the desire to leave home and make some of the sacrifices that the game demands.

When you make it to the big leagues, you're competing against the most talented players in the world. You don't become a star just because you want to be one. You have to sweat. You have to bleed. You must refuse to quit even though everything inside of you is crying for you to throw up your hands.

That's the same way I approached third base. I always felt it wasn't good enough merely to be a good hitter. The truly good player helps his team as much in the field as he does at the plate.

The key to becoming a good fielder is the same as becoming a good hitter. Work...work...work.

All the time till I signed professionally, I had played shortstop. When I started to play for a living, I realized I was too slow to play the position at that level.

Third base came somewhat naturally to me. But I had to work at it constantly to perform at the level I expected of myself.

I had coaches hit me hundreds of grounders every day. I wanted to learn every hop so that I could see it in my sleep. I wanted to know how every infield played so that I knew if I could cheat a step back or to either side.

I refused to play a ground ball off to the side if at all possible. I see a lot of third basemen today playing grounders off to their sides. If that ball bounces off their glove, it winds up out in left field. Now you've got your pitcher in trouble and the whole inning takes on a different look.

I don't care how hard a ball is hit, a third baseman must get in front of it. He has to at least knock it down. Even if he doesn't field the ball cleanly, he can still throw most runners out at first base.

Hoot Evers once complimented me and I've never forgotten.

"Kell is black and blue and bruised all over," he told a reporter, "from balls bouncing off of every part of his body. But you can't hit one by him. He's a brick wall. Those bruises are like medals. And he's a general when it comes to collecting them."

That's how I made it to the big leagues. That's how I worked my way toward becoming a .300 hitter in just my fourth season. And that's how I made my first All-Star team in my first season with Detroit. The game was at Wrigley field. Charlene and I were so excited. I didn't think there could be a bigger thrill in the game.

I was in my fourth big league season. I was hitting .300 at the time and I shouldn't have felt apprehensive. I was more nervous, though, than a young daddy at the birth of his first child. This was the All-Star Game and every big name in both leagues was going to be there.

I had the jitters till I finally walked into that American League clubhouse and saw all the players I competed against every day.

"Let's jump on them for four runs in the first inning and then watch them quit," Lou Boudreau cracked.

But it was Ted Williams who tried to settle me down in his own way.

"Aw, Kell will strike out to start the game," he joked, "but we'll still come back to slap four on them."

Nobody tested Ted Williams. Especially not a four-year player who was making his first All-Star appearance.

"How do you figure that?" I asked him.

In that bar room bellow that really was a sign he liked the person he was talking to, Williams responded, "Because Ewell Blackwell is pitching. He's taller than the flag pole. He throws the ball from down around his knees. He doesn't throw a pitch higher than the top of your kneecap. And he throws bullets. They explode. Watch out for shrapnel."

Of course, I had never seen Ewell Blackwell before. To myself, though, I said there was no way he was going to strike me out.

Blackwell needed only three pitches to make Williams a prophet. I was in pretty good company, though. Before the first inning was over, Blackwell also had struck out Joe DiMaggio and Lou Boudreau.

The next time up, I promised myself I would not strike out. I didn't care if I had to jump in front of a pitch. I dug in so close to the plate, I had to be outside of the batter's box. I fouled off a couple before grounding out to third. It wasn't a hit, but I didn't wind up swinging at air.

Once the game got going, I honestly felt like I belonged there. All the players made me feel like I was really one of them. We didn't win easily, but we did win, 2-1. It was the first of my six straight All-Star appearances and nine overall.

In 1946, I worked awfully hard to prove I could play on an All-Star level. I had to prove it to myself and also to all the Detroit fans who supported me right from the start. I finished with a .322 overall batting average. I struck out just 20 times and turned myself into a pretty good third baseman with only seven errors.

Even though I had made the All-Star team, when I came back in 1947 I felt I had to prove myself all over again. I had to prove the previous season was not a one-year fluke.

I was on a mission. The only way to accomplish it was to stay in that lineup every day. I played in all but two games and hit .320. I also finished with 93 runs batted in, which was pretty good for a second-place hitter.

After that season, I wasn't totally convinced I could hit .300 every year. I had no doubt, though, that I was an established major league player. I knew what I could do. I knew I would not allow anyone to come along and snatch my job away from me. I knew I never had another worry about playing major league baseball. I never felt cocky, but I felt awfully sure of myself.

From a personal standpoint, 1948 turned out to be the worst year of my career. I still kept my .300 string alive with a .304 mark, but I was limited to just 92 games because of two injuries, both at the hands of the Yankees.

In July I broke my wrist on a fastball from Vic Raschi. I was out for nearly four weeks and figured I could salvage the season in the last two months.

The next visit to Yankee Stadium squished that dream. Late in August a bad-hop grounder off Joe DiMaggio's bat finished my season. I suffered a broken jaw. I couldn't even smile when I recalled those words my father had told my mother about what I would do if a ground shot had been hit my way. I tried to come back late in the season. My strength had been drained, though, and I had to wait till the next year.

Once again, I felt I had to prove something. I had to prove I could bounce back from a few bad breaks and still be the same player I had worked so hard to become.

With a lot more sweat and a few good breaks, 1949 turned out to be quite a memorable season for me. In fact, I have a silver bat to prove it.

Kell's parents (Clyde and Alma) never missed a game in which George played as a youngster and often traveled to St. Louis to watch their son in the major leagues.

The Kell boys were quite a trio. George (left) and Everett Lee (Skeeter, center) both played in the major leagues. Frank (right) might have made it but was killed in service shortly after the conclusion of World War II.

George Kell was the All-American red-haired boy on graduation day from Swifton High School.

George broke into the major leagues with the old Philadelphia Athletics under the ownership of Connie Mack who also served as manager.

Once Kell was traded to the Tigers, he made Detroit his second home for the rest of his life.

Charlene and George Kell were childhood
sweethearts and celebrated their 50th
wedding anniversary before Charlene died.

Kell only has to walk a few blocks to visit the first real home that his mother and father had in Swifton when George was just a boy.

The Kell family (Charlene, George, Jr., Terrie and George) were the toast of Detroit when George played for the Tigers.

It was a glorious gathering of the Kell family in 1983 at Cooperstown when George was inducted into Baseball's Hall of Fame.

Besides Hall of Famer Stan Musial, Kell is the only former player to serve on the board of directors of a major league club. The former Detroit Tigers' board included (from lower center to left) Tom Monaghan, Bo Schembechler, George Griffith, Doug Dawson, Kell and Jim Campbell.

George's prayers to God were answered
when he married Carolyn in 1994.

Over the years, Kell has carefully nurtured the crops that have grown on his farm land in his beloved hometown of Swifton.

Nothing is closer to Kell's heart than the Swifton United Methodist Church of which Kell has been a member and served since his boyhood.

The lemonade stand in "downtown" Swifton
is a welcome stop on a hot muggy day.

The Swifton Community Center now stands
at the center of downtown where there used
to be several movie theaters.

The George Kell Park in nearby Newport is now home to the American Legion team where Kell got his start in organized baseball.

The George Kell Motor Company, now owned by George Kell, Jr. and his partner, is now a landmark in Newport and is one of Arkansas' most successful automobile dealerships.

The lighted diamond in George Kell Park brings back
a lot of memories for the man after whom it is named.

CHAPTER NINE

BREAKING THE COLOR BARRIER

I t took baseball more than a half century to address one of its most serious shortcomings in history. But it finally took a step in the right direction with the signing of Jackie Robinson in 1947.

Like the rest of the nation, baseball was socked by extremely trying circumstances during World War II. Many of the game's veteran stars and a whole lot of its promising young players were called into the service.

Through no fault of its own, the game had become diluted. It had been weakened, however, for the right reason. The world was at war. Baseball certainly could not come before our national interests.

Baseball must accept responsibility for diluting its quality through a conscious decision of its own, however. In fact, today we look back and wonder why it ever took so long to allow black players to take their proper place in the major leagues.

Even to this day I am shocked that somebody along the way didn't have the guts to stand up and say that it is flat out wrong not to let a man play major league baseball simply because of the color of his skin. That's unforgivable! There is no excuse that can ever justify that sin.

Now there are some black ball players whom I don't particularly like. I feel the same way about a lot of white ball players. I don't like the way certain players act and ignore the fact that they represent major league baseball.

That has absolutely nothing to do with the color of a man's skin, though. A fool is a fool whether he's white, black, green or purple.

Monte Irvin was a star in the old Negro Leagues before he was allowed to play in the majors. He wound up making the Hall of Fame.

"I don't know why they didn't allow the black players to come up earlier," I told him. "If they had, I might not have had a job. There were so many good ones."

He assured me that America was cheated out of enjoying a countless number of good black ball players.

We had trouble drawing fans in Philadelphia when I played for the Athletics. Twice I went out to the Negro Leagues games because I wanted the chance to see Satchel Paige pitch.

There wasn't a seat to be found. Both times the park was packed because there were so many good black players. Some of those teams may have been better than a few in the major leagues. That tells you how short-sighted baseball was.

Stories have been told that Satchel Paige threw the ball harder than any human being who ever put on a pair of spikes. Once he finally was allowed to play in the majors, I batted against him a couple of times. But he must have been 50 years old at the time. He was only a shell of the pitcher that he used to be.

Baseball hurt itself with its reluctance to invite blacks to play in the big leagues long before 1947. We robbed people from seeing one of the greatest pitchers of all time...flat out robbed them.

Baseball history books might really sparkle if the black players had been allowed to play earlier than 1947. We lost a lot of good players for no reason at all.

If Josh Gibson had been half as good as people say he was, we might have missed out on seeing the greatest player in history. People who saw both of them play say that he was twice the player Roy Campenella was. And Roy Campenella was one of the best players I ever saw.

I'm not sure if baseball imitates life or life imitates baseball. We all know what had happened up until 1947 was wrong. It took far too long to correct this unthinkable practice. Thank God, though, it was eventually addressed. Once baseball took that one big step to open its doors to all qualified players, it created a bigger change for making the game stronger than by having all its stars return from the war.

Can anyone even imagine baseball history without Hank Aaron? What about Willie Mays? Bob Gibson? Reggie Jackson? Willie McCovey? Frank Robinson? Willie Stargell? Joe Morgan?

The list goes on and on and on. Look at all of the rosters on today's clubs. Forget all about the history part. What we did was wrong. And it took more than 50 years to fix it.

Long before the Brooklyn Dodgers broke the color line and brought Jackie Robinson into the National League, I was bothered by the fact that blacks were prohibited to play major league baseball. When I first made it to the Athletics, I remember talking to my father about that.

"Why can't a black man play ball in the major leagues if he's good enough to compete?" I asked him.

Even though my father was a quiet and gentle person, inside he was outraged that such an injustice was allowed to go on for so long. My father was a very religious person. He believed that all people are God's children. He knew that God never paid any attention to the color of a man's skin. God loves everybody the same. If God made all people equal, then everyone should be given the same opportunities.

That's the way I was brought up to live my life and that's the way I believe we all are supposed to live.

When you were a boy growing up in the South in the 1920s and 1930s, racial segregation was all around you. It was impossible to ignore. But my mother and father taught me and my brothers that all people are created equal. Even though we weren't old enough to understand some of the things happening around us, it was impossible to ignore the different standards for black people and white people.

My first real exposure to black people came way back in Swifton when I was just a boy. And I hold nothing but good memories about all of the people I met.

One of my uncles owned a farm at that time. One of the workers he hired was a black man, and I don't remember the man's name, but I do remember my uncle saying one time that "that black worker is one of the hardest working hands I ever did hire."

My father hired a black porter who worked in his barber shop for many years. I used to joke around with him in the shop while he shined shoes so bright they'd make your eyes squint.

For Sunday church services, he would press trousers for all the men in town. All the men wanted to look their best for Sunday services. Daddy's porter always had about a dozen to do on Saturdays.

When I was a youngster some time during the early 1930s, the railroad line decided to replace the tracks that ran straight through the heart of Swifton. Those tracks had been a part of the town for as long as anyone could remember. The railroad section crew had to keep those tracks in excellent working condition. That line was a prime stretch for transporting a variety of goods throughout the whole state and up into Missouri.

Finally there came a time when some of the tracks needed to be replaced. During the summer, the railroad sent a crew of about 50 men to rip out those old tracks and lay new ones. They spent almost three months on that job working from Walnut Ridge through Swifton and all the way south to Newport.

It gets so hot and humid in the summer in Swifton that sweating almost becomes a regular pastime. That crew lived out of railroad bunk cars parked along the tracks. They didn't even have fans to keep cool. My mother made some extra money that summer by taking in the wash for all the men on the crew.

There were about six or eight black workers and one of them spotted me carrying my baseball glove to the field one day.

"Do you boys play ball nearby?" he asked.

"Everyday, right behind the school," I told him.

"Do you mind if we come over and play you boys?" he asked.

"If you have a team, just come on over any day when you're finished with your work," I said. "It's right up behind the school. We've got enough gloves and bats and balls for everybody."

So every day at four o'clock when they were finished laying track, that black crew walked over to the field in their overalls and we played ball till it was dark.

They were grown men. Some of them played pretty well and we had some fine games. But not a word was said in the community about us playing that black team. We wound up having a good summer with some different competition. They got the chance to get in some baseball and discover that not everyone in the South thought the same.

For the most part, I'm sorry to say, the South at that time was racially segregated. There were certain parts of the South where a get-together like this would have been grounds for a hanging. But nobody in town said one word about it. Everybody just went about their business and we kept on playing ball.

There was a young black kid named Tommy Dedman who played ball up at the school with us every day. Tommy was a good little player. In fact, he probably played a little better than some of the rest of our gang. He showed up every day like everybody else. We'd flip the bat to choose up sides. The color of his skin was never any big deal to us.

We never thought anything about it until one day we decided to walk about three miles out of town to play some kids from a country school in a ball game.

All of us boys from Swifton, including Tommy, walked on out there to show them how the real players from the "big city" played the game. Just as we were getting ready to start, I remember an older man walking up to the field.

"He's not going to play," he said as he pointed at Tommy Dedman.

All of us were a little confused about exactly what was happening. We all quickly agreed, though, that if Tommy wasn't going to play, then none of us were.

Not a whole lot more was said. We simply gathered up all of our bats and balls and walked on back to Swifton. We went behind the school on the field and played our usual pick-up game.

That was probably the first time I was ever directly exposed to real segregation. I didn't understand it. Obviously, I didn't like it. But I really didn't know how to go about changing anything.

I do feel I tried to enact some change years later when I served on the Swifton Board of Education. For years, even after I had grown, black students were not allowed to attend school in Swifton once they reached high school age. After finishing grade school, black students were bussed to the high school in Tuckerman.

That made no sense at all. Not only did it cost the school system money to bus the students, it wasn't morally right. We got busy and changed the rules. The high school in Swifton became integrated just like all the other schools.

I was playing for the Tigers when Jackie Robinson broke in with the Dodgers in 1947. I know how tough it was for me to break into the major leagues even during the war years. I can't imagine how tough it was for Robinson or any of those early black players.

To tell the truth, I'm not sure if I would have had the strength to endure all the tests they had to go through and still perform at the major league level.

The arrival of the black players changed the course of baseball for the rest of history. The game would never be the same. It would be better.

I wasn't directly involved with the history making of 1947. I was merely a ball player trying to improve my career. I honestly never paid much attention to what other players were doing other than when I was playing against them. I kept my focus on trying to beat them before they could get to me.

I am happy and proud, though, to have been part of baseball when the color line finally was broken. In some small way I feel like I was a little part of history. For sure, I felt awfully proud of the way Jackie Robinson handled himself. Not only as a ball player, but also as a man.

I never really did get the chance to know Jackie Robinson. The only time we met was in 1948. I received the most votes for the All-Star Game and he was second. They took a picture of us together. I was proud to be coupled with him.

Robinson played in the National League so I really never had any contact with him. Larry Doby was the first black player in the American League with Cleveland and I got to know him a little.

Being a player, especially back then, I stuck pretty much to my own business. I didn't pay much attention to all the political stuff that was going around. So I don't truly don't remember a lot of the verbal abuse players like Robinson and Doby had to endure.

They wouldn't have said anything if it hadn't happened, though. I'm sure there were people in the stands and some players who were capable of sinking that low. I simply don't remember.

I do know from first-hand experience that Larry Doby was one terrific ball player. He had power and he could go get a ball. He led the American League in homers twice. He also led the league in runs batted in once.

All the talk I remember about Robinson is how good a player he was. He wasn't just a black player...he was a great player. He could do everything...run, hit, field, throw. He led the National League in hitting after being up for only two years. And from what I was told, there was no greater competitor.

After I started to play on teams with black players, I do remember some of the insulting double standards they had to endure. Once I discovered what was going on, I was appalled to think things like that were allowed to happen in the major leagues or anywhere in the United States.

It was sickening.

For instance, when the team bus brought us from the airport to the hotel, I noticed there always were a couple of cars waiting.

All of the white players would gather their belongings and head for their rooms. Keys were waiting for them at the front desk.

Not the black players. They weren't allowed to stay in all the hotels. Those cars at the curb were waiting to take them to the other side of town. They would be housed in the homes of black people.

It was the same way in spring training. While the white players were housed in the team hotel headquarters, clubs found families with homes on the other side of town for the black players to stay.

I said to myself, "I can't believe this." A player couldn't do anything about it, but as God is my witness, if I owned a major league team and a hotel said the black players couldn't stay there I'd pull the whole team out and find somewhere else to spend my money.

I still wonder to this day why baseball ever allowed this practice to go on. It was shameful and it was wrong. That kind of thing made me sick to my stomach. Thank God those days are past us. Hopefully we have learned something from our mistakes.

The first black teammate of mine was Minnie Minoso at the Chicago White Sox. Minnie was a terrific player and an even better person. We became good friends the first day we met.

Of course, that didn't require much. Minnie Minoso was one of the finest human beings anyone ever had the privilege to meet. I can't think of one person who wasn't proud to call that man a friend.

"Hey, George Kell...George Kell," he yelled at me the first day I showed up at Chicago. "I was a little baby boy in Cuba when I heard you playing ball."

He put his hand down toward his knee to indicate how small he had been at the time.

"You were in the big leagues when I was just this big," he said with that smile of his that made your belly break out with a bigger laugh than you thought it could hold.

"Minoso," I told him, "you're older than I am now."

Then he started to laugh.

"No, no, George Kell," he said. "I was just a little baby boy. I always liked you. You were my idol."

How could anyone get mad at someone like that?

"You're the only man I know who played in the big leagues and drew his pension at the same time," I tell him today whenever we meet. Then he breaks out in that same infectious laugh that has made him so precious for all these years.

To this day, I honestly don't know how old Minnie Minoso is. I'm not sure he even knows. All I know is that he was one tough ball player who could run, throw, field and hit.

He played the game hard. He didn't know how to play it any other way. He was fearless. There was no in-between with Minnie Minoso and there was never any belly-aching. He played baseball the way it's meant to be played.

Both of us made the All-Star team the year the game was played in Chicago. After I was finished with batting practice, I was walking up the third base line. Minnie had his glove and was about to run out to left field. He grabbed me and put his arm around my shoulders.

"How much longer are you going to play, old man?" he asked me and poked me in the ribs before running off to shag flies.

"Your pension ought to shoot up a little now that you made the All-Star team," I joked back.

A few weeks after the game, I received a letter from a fan. I have no idea whether the writer was a white man or a black man. In his letter he said he thought "it was the greatest thing in the world to see Minnie Minoso and George Kell walking down the third base line laughing with their arms around each other."

At the time Minoso and I did that, I never even gave it a second thought. But that letter meant a lot to me.

When I look back, it still saddens me to think it took baseball so long to do the right thing. It should have been done right from the start. I believe baseball still must continue to work at improving its relationship with players of every nationality, not just the blacks.

Baseball has been fortunate to have drawn a wealth of players from South America. It's critical that the game continues to find ways not only to capitalize on talent from around the world but also to function as a leader in human relations.

We all must remember that baseball is often used as a yardstick for our national conscience. If we make a mistake in our own backyard it's felt in the living rooms of people all over the country.

I can't say that I played a major role in turning the tide on our past mistakes. I will say that I am proud that I was around when baseball took its first steps toward correcting certain injustices that were allowed to exist for far too long.

It was an exciting time. Now it's time to make things even better. The history books will forever be a little brighter with the inclusion of players of all nationalities.

CHAPTER TEN

CONFIDENCE AND A CUP OF COFFEE

Sometimes if you just keep your eyes and ears open and your mouth shut, one of the greatest lessons you'll ever learn will fall right into your lap.

Even in a place like Tuscaloosa, Alabama.

Years later, Bear Bryant made Tuscaloosa one of the most famous college towns in the country.

For me, it had a special significance even before The Bear made it the football capital of the South.

On my way to spring training in 1949, Tuscaloosa became the unlikely city where I picked up one of the greatest batting tips I ever learned in my life.

It didn't happen on the diamond. It didn't even happen anywhere near a ball park. It took place in the coffee shop of the Tuscaloosa Hotel. I learned right there that confidence in your ability to hit in the big leagues is just as important as your God-given talent.

At the time, I didn't fully appreciate the lesson. Before the season was over, though, I understood it as much as The Bear's boys knew the end around. I carried that lesson throughout the rest of my career. It helped to make me a better ball player and also gave me a finer appreciation for the gift God had given me.

And it all happened in the Hotel Tuscaloosa, just a couple of blocks from the University of Alabama, in March, 1949.

In those days, most of the players drove down to Florida for spring training. Tuscaloosa seemed about half-way to Lakeland from our home in Swifton. So Charlene, the kids and I would spend a night there.

Johnny Sain was from Walnut Ridge, Arkansas, not too far from Swifton. I had told John about the hotel and he began to stop there on his trip to Florida.

After spending the night, Charlene decided she did not want breakfast the next morning. So I decided to run downstairs for a quick cup of coffee and some toast before finishing the trip for the start of another season.

When I got to the coffee shop, Sain already was sitting at a table and he wasn't alone. With him were Red Schoendienst and the great Stan Musial who were on their way to the St. Louis Cardinals' camp in St. Petersburg. To me, that table had the grace of royalty. I was delighted when they motioned me over to join them.

Most of the conversation was small talk. We talked about what we had done over the winter and what we wanted to accomplish during the season.

Everybody contributed. Then Musial started to talk about hitting. When Stan Musial decides to talk about hitting, only a fool doesn't hang on to every word he says.

Stan had a way of making hitting seem so simple. For him it was. For me and all the rest of us, it took a lot of work. Then he laid something on us that I remember to this day.

"I've reached the point in my career that when I go to spring training, I know I'm going to hit somewhere between .320 and .340 for the season," he said.

Stan was not bragging. He was good enough to back it up and then some. He had reached the point where his confidence would not allow him to fall short of his goals.

I went back upstairs to my room thinking that was the most amazing thing about hitting I had ever heard in my life. The fact that a man knew before the season started that he would finish somewhere between .320 and .340 actually staggered my imagination.

He was talking about confidence. A player simply cannot become a good hitter without it.

To imagine that a man could feel so sure of himself that he could do it year after year proved to me how critical confidence is to the great hitters.

Throughout that entire 1949 season, I kept thinking about what Musial had said. It wasn't until the season was over and I realized that I had won the American League batting championship that I fully appreciated what that lesson truly means.

After finishing at .343 and winning the title over Ted Williams, I made up my mind that there was no way any pitchers could keep me from hitting somewhere between .310 and .325 every year. Once I set my mind to that, when I left Swifton for spring training every year, I knew I was leaving as a bona fide .300 hitter. And when I returned home in the fall, I knew I was going back as one of the major leagues' best.

I had learned how to become a .300 hitter. I could bunt. I could hit-and-run. I could pull the ball. I could hit it to right. I never was very fast, but I knew how to pull the third baseman into playing a step closer. Then I'd move in on top of the plate, wait for an inside pitch and slash it past him.

I realized I never would be as great a hitter as Stan Musial was. Guys like Musial and Williams and DiMaggio and Mantle were in a class of their own.

But I also realized that if I concentrated hard enough and played to the best of my ability, I knew I could make that All-Star team every year.

Once I developed the confidence to believe in my own ability, I honestly believe I became a better ball player. And it all began over a cup of coffee with Stan Musial in Tuscaloosa, Alabama.

I was fairly consistent right through the entire 1949 season. I never gave much thought to winning the batting title, though, because Williams had come back from the war with the usual spit in his eye.

Ted Williams was the best hitter I ever saw. He could hit .340 just like setting the watch on his wrist. I'd push myself to stay three or four points behind him while he was making it look so easy. It almost looked like he was teasing the rest of us hitters. I always thought he was right on the edge of piling up ten hits in his next fifteen at bats to make a joke out of the batting race.

It wasn't until after the All-Star break that anybody even mentioned my name in the same breath with the batting title.

My locker was located next to Hoot Evers'. Hoot was a player tougher than leather. He also was one of my best friends in Detroit.

"If it wasn't for Williams, you'd lead the league in hitting this year," Hoot told me. "Somewhere along the line, though, he's going to put on a rush and blow everybody away."

I didn't argue with Hoot. I thought the same thing was going to happen.

The season wore down to the end of August when I realized I was trailing Williams by only a couple of points. That's the first time I actually let myself think about the fact that I even had a chance of winning the title.

In the last couple of weeks of the season, I got hot and piled up a carload of hits to make the race tight. I was one point behind Williams going into the last day of the season. On that Sunday in Detroit, I received a call from Charlene when I arrived at the clubhouse. She already had returned to Swifton and had just gotten home from church.

"You're going to lead the league in hitting," she told me. "I know you can. All you need is a couple of hits."

I told Hoot Evers what Charlene had said.

"She's right," Hoot said. "George, you are going to lead the league. You have the confidence. You are determined. All you need are two hits."

Charlene and Hoot were two of the people I relied most on.

"How do you know that?" I asked him. "What if Williams goes out and gets four?"

That didn't seem to bother Hoot.

"I just know it," he said. "Go on out and get two hits and you're going to lead the league. Get them your first times up."

For whatever reason, I thought maybe Charlene and Hoot knew something I didn't know. The only thing I knew for sure was that we were playing Cleveland and Bob Lemon was starting for the Indians.

I always felt that Bob Feller was the toughest pitcher I ever faced. Lemon was a close second. Together, they were a one-two knockout punch that floored almost every American League hitter.

The first time up, I rifled a two-base hit down into the left field corner. The second time up, I lined a single to left.

I had gotten those two hits that I needed. Before I came to bat for the third time, though, I heard a ball exploding into a glove in the Cleveland bullpen. It sounded like bombs were going off.

Thump. Thump. Thump.

It was Feller warming up that fastball of his. Just the sound made a lot of hitters shiver. I remember thinking to myself that I had gotten by Lemon with a couple of hits. Now I was going to have to face Feller. That was always as much fun as getting a tooth pulled without any pain killer.

The Indians needed a win to finish third and pick up a few extra dollars. If they couldn't do it with Lemon and Feller then they couldn't do it at all.

The first time up against Feller I drew a walk. Then I faced him in the last of the seventh inning and he struck me out with that "thump, thump, thump."

"I told you two hits would do it," Evers told me. "Now get out of the lineup and go home. You've got the title won."

I wasn't in the position to simply take myself out of the lineup. Besides, we still had a chance to win the game.

Communications in those days weren't as sophisticated as they are today with television and computers. The Red Sox were playing in New York and I had no idea what Williams was doing.

We were trailing when it got to the ninth, so we had to bat in the last half of the inning. I was the fourth scheduled hitter. I was sitting on a two-for-three day and I thought to myself that it wouldn't bother me a lick if I didn't have to bat again.

Dick Wakefield was sent up to pinch hit to lead off the ninth. He singled on the first pitch. The next batter popped out and I jumped out of the dugout for the on deck circle.

As Eddie Lake settled in the batter's box, I heard Joe Ginsberg yelling at me from our dugout.

"Come here...come here," Ginsberg shouted.

Right at that moment, Lake hit a picture-perfect two-hop ground ball to Ray Boone at short. It was one of those grounders your mother could have stuffed in her back pocket. Boone moved quickly toward second, stepped on the bag and fired to first to complete the double play.

The game was over. I threw my bat up in the air as high as I could. I didn't know for sure, but I thought I had a chance at the title.

Lyall Smith was the baseball writer for *The Detroit Free Press*. He was a good friend of mine and had called down to the dugout to let Red Rolfe know that if I didn't bat again, the title was mine. Lyall had called New York to find out that Williams had gone hitless.

Ginsberg was trying to let me know he was going to hit for me. Everybody on the bench knew that if I didn't go to bat, the title was mine.

After the game ended, I raced into the clubhouse and called Charlene. When I told her what had happened, she began to cry. It was a great moment for us to share.

As soon as I got off the phone, a lot of the writers asked if I had thought about not going to the plate in the ninth inning. I never really had a choice. The last play happened so fast that there wasn't a chance for anybody to make a decision.

I can't express how I felt when the news finally sunk in. Winning the American League batting title is one thing. Beating out Ted Williams to do it made it even more special.

I wanted that title real bad. Not just for me, but also for my father. He helped me so much when I was just a kid. I do remember thinking that the title belonged as much to him as it did to me.

It was the second Silver Bat I had won in my career. I received one for hitting .396 at Lancaster to lead all of the minor leagues. I gave both bats to the Hall of Fame in Cooperstown.

Certainly I would have traded all the Silver Bats in the world to have had the chance to play in a World Series. For an individual honor, though, I couldn't have been more proud.

I felt now that I had finally earned my place among the league's best. When I headed home to Swifton that fall, I knew I would arrive as the batting champion of the American League. And to make that off-season even more special, my daughter, Terrie, was born the first month we got back.

From the first year I came to Detroit, I never hit below .300. The Tigers treated me very well with my salary. The first few years there I received a $2,500 bonus after every season. They also raised my salary each year. I was earning $27,500 when I led the league in hitting.

At the end of that season, Mr. Trautman (Tiger general manager) offered me a contract for $37,500. I never had a problem signing any of my contracts, but I told him I thought that was a little low for someone who had just won the batting title and plays every day.

"Well, what do you think you deserve?" he asked.

My confidence at that point had sailed to an all-time high.

"I feel like I'm the best infielder in the league," I told him confidently without bragging.

"I play every day. I hit more than any of them. I make the All-Star team every year."

He listened carefully. He did not argue.

"That's fair enough," he said. "Who makes the most?"

In those days, contract figures weren't as much common knowledge as they are today.

"(Phil) Rizzuto told me he's making $50,000 a year," I told him.

Trautman never flinched, but he was slightly stunned.

"Whew," he said. "I don't know if we can afford that. But I agreed to it, so let me get things going."

About a week later, he called me in Swifton.

"Your contract is in the mail," he said. "Rizzuto is not making $50,000. He was just pulling your leg. He's making $45,000 and if that's agreeable to you, that's what you'll get. But you better have a big year to earn it."

I signed that contract and that's the figure I made each year for the rest of my career.

There isn't a man who played this game who doesn't believe he's worth more money than he's making. That's the way it should be. It keeps a player hungry.

When I got up to that level, though, the money honestly didn't mean as much to me as what I did on the field. I wasn't doing it just for the money. I wanted to be the best player I could be.

With that batting title in my back pocket, I knew I was on my way. All I wanted to do was to play every day. Everything else would take care of itself. I knew what I could do. I was confident in my ability.

I suppose that confidence began to blossom several years before somewhere on a diamond down in Swifton. It sure did get the final boost from Stan Musial. And a cup of coffee in Tuscaloosa.

CHAPTER ELEVEN

THE GREEN MONSTER AND TED

Winning the batting title did not put any extra pressure on me. If it did anything, it drove me to show everybody it was no fluke.

Players just don't come along and steal a title away from Ted Williams. He made everybody earn it. That's what I felt I had done. I had earned it.

With the kind of money I was earning then, there was no way I could let the Tigers down. They had rewarded me with their confidence. I had to repay that with consistency.

In 1950, I had an even better year than I did the previous season. I should have won a second straight batting title, but wound up second to Billy Goodman.

Up until the second half of the season, Goodman had been a part-time player for Boston. At the All-Star Game in Comiskey Park, though, Williams ran into the left field fence and broke his elbow. Goodman was moved to left and finished the season playing every day.

Up until the last ten days of the season, there was doubt whether he would get enough plate appearances to qualify for the batting title. That's when (Boston Manager) Joe McCarthy moved him to the leadoff spot so that he could qualify.

He qualified and finished with a .354 average on 150 hits in 424 times up in 110 games. I played every game and finished at .340. I led the league with 641 at bats, 218 hits and 56 doubles. Nobody's had that many doubles since then. With artificial turf today, they ought to get a hundred.

I also had a career-high 114 runs and 101 runs batted in. I was confident about every aspect of my game. I committed just nine errors and struck out only eighteen times.

I've always been proud of the fact that I rarely struck out. I struck out just 287 times in my career and never more than 37 in one season. If you put the ball in play, something has to happen. If nothing else, at least you can move up a runner.

The consistency I tried so hard to establish was there. Except for Williams, DiMaggio, Berra, Mantle and a few guys like that, I was confident I could play with anybody. In 1951 I batted .319 and led the league with 191 hits and 36 doubles. I made the All-Star team every year I played in Detroit. The 1951 game was special for me, though, because my mother and father came to Briggs Stadium to watch. I got lucky and hit a home run.

I never wanted to play anywhere but Detroit and never even dreamed I wouldn't get the chance to finish my career there. Then on June 3, 1952, I was shocked beyond belief when I was traded to the Boston Red Sox.

Even more than my trade to Detroit six years earlier, I was confused by the deal. I wasn't angry. By this time I realized that anything was possible in baseball.

I just couldn't figure out why it happened. I was in the lineup every day. I hit .300 and made the All-Star team every year. What does a player have to do to make himself secure in his city?

The deal was a whopper. Dizzy Trout, Johnny Lipon, Hoot Evers and I were sent to Boston. Walt Dropo, Bill Wight, Fred Hatfield, Johnny Pesky and Don Lenhardt wound up in Detroit.

The Tigers were in last place at the time and headed nowhere. Charlie Gehringer was the Tiger General Manager.

"We had to do something to shake up the club," Gehringer explained to me. "There was no way we wanted to move you. But every time we got close to a trade (Joe) Cronin (Boston General Manager) said there's no deal if Kell isn't part of it. He was adamant that you be part of the deal."

I suppose that should have made me feel good. At the time, though, I don't think I was smiling.

The Tigers were in Philadelphia when the deal was announced. We had finished a series in Washington and arrived the night before starting a series with the Athletics.

Ironically, the Athletics had just called up my brother, Skeeter, from the minor leagues. We were looking forward to playing against each other in the major leagues for the first time.

My mother and father were really excited about this series and decided to drive up from Swifton. They drove through Detroit to pick up Charlene and the kids. We all spent the night at Skeeter's place and enjoyed a little family reunion.

Skeeter joked about how he was going to show me up in the big time the next night. I was enjoying myself like everyone else, but I made a promise to myself that he was not going to show me up. I had been up in the big leagues for a long time and I was not going to let a rookie show me up. Even if that rookie happened to be my brother.

But it was a generally great time. I had not told anyone on the Tigers that I was spending the night with my family. No one on the club knew how to get hold of me.

The trade was announced at three o'clock the next afternoon right before I showed up at Shibe Park. As soon as I arrived, Red Rolfe said they had been looking for me all day.

"We spent the night with my brother," I told him. "He just got called up to the Athletics. My parents are here, my wife is here and we've just had a great time."

Red's jaw must have dropped to the tip of his spikes when I told him that.

"You're not going to play, son," he told me. "We just traded you to Boston."

Later that season I played against Skeeter. I was looking forward to that first meeting more for my parents than myself. Baseball is funny that way. It doesn't stop in the middle of a season for any type of family affair.

Joe Cronin actually had wanted me in Boston for that night's game. I called to tell him I couldn't make it until the next day. He told me to be on the midnight train and ready to go the next afternoon at Fenway Park.

"Mr. Cronin, I have to be honest," I told him. "You know I did not want to be traded. I love Detroit. It's just like home to me. If I have to be traded, though, I want it to be Boston more than any other city."

He understood. He explained how much I would love Boston and playing in Fenway every day.

So the next day I was at Fenway playing the Cleveland Indians. I hit one ball over that Green Monster in left field and another one off of it for a double.

For a right-handed hitter without much power like myself, Boston is a great place to play. It's not much more than a long pop fly to hit that wall. It stands out there like some barker at a carnival just daring you to hit it. It stands so high it makes you feel like you can just reach out and touch it.

After I was traded to Boston, before every game I felt like I would hit that wall at least once. If you train yourself right, you can make that wall your friend. Even if you can't hit it all the time, it gives you the feeling that you can. It's more of a confidence builder than a hanging curveball. Just don't let it trick you, because it can also be the devil.

As soon as I got there, Joe Cronin had a long talk with me about all the little nooks and crannies and demons that live in old Fenway Park.

"George, do not let that wall get in your eyes," he told me. "I traded for you because you can hit to all fields. You can hit and run and put the ball where you want to. Don't try to pull everything over that devil out there. Make the wall work for you. Don't you become a slave to it."

That left a lasting impression on me. I didn't change my style of hitting unless we really needed a long ball late in a game. I hit one ball over the monster in the ninth inning to win a game. I simply squared around and was determined that I was either going to put one over it or off of it.

But that big green thing still remains a temptress even today.

I wound up hitting a career-high twelve home runs in my only full season in Boston in 1953. And I had the monster to thank for it.

I settled into Boston quicker than I thought I would. I always enjoyed visiting the city. Living there was a good feeling. I've always enjoyed walking through every city I visited. Boston is one of the best walking towns in the league. Every place you go you bump into a little piece of history.

It's a beautiful blend of old and new. There are so many old red brick buildings. The streets are clean and people walk around downtown all day and all night. There are so many colleges throughout the whole area that there always seems to be a charge of energy.

My wife and I took advantage of everything in Boston. We drove to Cap Cod. We visited Harvard. We went to the Boston Pops several times.

Boston fans are a lot like those in Detroit. They follow all their teams with a religious passion. They're good fans and appreciate good plays whether it's from the Red Sox or an opposing team.

I was 31 years old when I played that full season in Boston and I appreciated the climate. As a player gets older, the heat zaps the energy out of you a lot quicker than it does younger players. Boston was just cool enough that I felt strong all the time. Especially night games. It's a great place for older players to go.

Of course, being traded to Boston gave me the opportunity to watch Ted Williams play every day. That was a privilege. Sometimes I felt like I was cheating the Red Sox. I should have paid the price of admission just to watch him hit every day. Even watching him take batting practice was a learning experience.

Ted had been called back into the service for the Korean War about two weeks after I arrived in Boston. When he returned, though, it was well worth the wait. There was nothing Ted Williams could not do with a bat. He was by far the best hitter I have ever seen.

We were playing a series in New York. I rode out to Yankee Stadium in a cab with Williams. He had been hit on the wrist and I know for a fact he was hurting. Whitey Ford was starting for the Yankees and it would have been a good time for Ted to rest his wrist against a tough lefty like Ford.

"I can play," he grumbled as we pulled up to the park. "I'll take Ford to left field all night."

He did and wound up getting three hits. He had supreme confidence in his ability.

Ted Williams was a tough, disciplined player who was all business once he walked onto that field. He never gave an inch and never asked for an inch. Yet he was one of the most generous men I ever met in sharing his baseball knowledge.

When Al Kaline broke in with the Tigers, he was one of the best looking young players to come into the league in a long time. Williams took a liking to Kaline. He loved Kaline's swing and his dedication to the game. Williams spent a lot of time talking hitting with Kaline when the Tigers and Red Sox played. Kaline gives Williams a lot of credit for his development as a hitter.

It didn't take a player with the talent of Kaline, though, to draw Ted's attention. If you wanted to talk about hitting, you could be a .220 hitter and Ted would talk till it was time to go to bed.

Everybody knew that Ted hated pitchers. He would help hitters by telling them what certain pitchers were going to try to do in certain situations.

"He's going to try to set you up with a certain pitch," he'd say. "You better hit him before he gets you too deep in the count. Hit him before he does."

He had hitting figured out to the bones. He was a scientist with the bat.

Ted Williams was a very tough man. He was strong physically and he was just as mentally tough. When he put his mind to something, he was going to get the job done and it would be done right. When it came to hitting, it seemed like Ted could almost will something to happen. Down deep, he was a gentleman. If he was your friend, he was behind you all the way.

I was honored that Ted welcomed me as soon as I got to Boston. He was a big booster of mine.

"You're going to love this park," he said. "It's a great place to play and you should have been playing here all the time."

I had been a little concerned that he might have been upset with me for costing him the Triple Crown when I beat him for the batting title in 1949. But he never said a word about it. He was always quick to give credit to players.

At the Hall of Fame ceremonies in 1997, all of us were waiting behind the stage to be introduced to the fans. Ted was there and still joked about that batting title race we had 47 years ago.

"Here's the man who beat me out of the Triple Crown in 1949," he said to all the other Hall of Famers.

I told Ted that for a long time I hadn't even realized that by not winning the batting title, he had lost the Triple Crown. I thought he was going to be upset.

"Hell no," Ted bellowed. "You beat me fair and square, the way you're supposed to. It was a great race. I loved it. I admired the way you stuck with me all the way. That's the way the game is supposed to be played. I'm glad I got the chance to play with you."

What bothered Williams was when players he thought should have been better didn't push themselves hard enough.

"He could be a better player if he applied himself," I heard him say of certain players.

I never wanted to leave Detroit. But I got the Green Monster, Ted Williams and all of that New England charm. I couldn't complain.

CHAPTER TWELVE

THE GOLDEN YEARS

Ted Williams was not the best ball player I ever saw. Without question he was, by far, the best hitter. I don't believe any human being ever came close to Williams' shadow as a hitter. And none ever will.

Williams was not the best all-around player. With the bat, though, he performed on a level that was far above where the rest of us operated.

If Williams couldn't do it with his bat, then it could not be done. He was the closest thing to perfection anyone has seen.

If all the rest of us major league hitters were beautiful pictures compared to those who didn't make it professionally, then Ted Williams as a hitter was a genuine piece of art. He might have been the purest hitter in the history of the game. If he wasn't, then whoever was could not have been human.

I was very lucky to have played in the big leagues during the period of history that I did. There probably isn't a former player who doesn't believe he took part in the most glorious niche of baseball history. That's the way it's supposed to be. A player is supposed to be proud of his time in the big leagues. Besides, it makes for good arguments and spikes life into the game.

So I might be a bit biased with my selection.

I've got a lot of ammunition on my side, though. Many baseball historians claim that the period right after World War II marked the beginning of baseball's Golden Era. I happen to agree. In fact, I'm not sure we'll ever witness that particular caliber of baseball ever again.

There was Ted Williams . . . Joe DiMaggio . . . Mickey Mantle . . . Jackie Robinson . . . Hank Aaron . . . Willie Mays . . . Stan Musial . . . Warren Spahn . . . Bob Feller . . . Yogi Berra . . . Duke Snider . . . Al

Kaline ... Pee Wee Reese ... Brooks Robinson ... Lou Boudreau. The list goes on and on.

Every era boasts its own cast of particularly talented players. I believe that the stars of any particular period would be superior to most of their peers regardless of the era in which they played.

For instance, Johnny Bench could have played in any era and still have been the Johnny Bench we all marveled at. So could have Joe Morgan and Reggie Jackson and Mike Schmidt and Brooks Robinson and Nolan Ryan and Dave Winfield and George Brett and a long litany of players.

The same holds true for today's superstars. Players like Ken Griffey, Jr. and Cal Ripken, Jr. and Barry Bonds and Frank Thomas and Alan Trammell and Lou Whitaker and Jack Morris and Randy Johnson and Kenny Lofton, to name just a few, would have starred in any era.

It wouldn't matter if they had played in 1920 or 1950 or 1990 or 20 years from now. They would be superior performers and leave their marks on the record books. Whatever it took to compete at the highest level, those kind of players would do it.

For sheer overall quality and crispness of play, though, I honestly do believe that those years from 1946 up into the early 1960s were the finest in the sport's history.

Certainly the game has changed. It's been improved in a variety of areas. More fans go to the park today than during any period of history. More games are televised now than ever before. I can sit in my den in Swifton and pick up three or four different games every night during the summer off of my satellite dish.

Playing conditions are so much better. Equipment has improved. There's no comparison between today's training programs and those from the past. Players are bigger, stronger and in far better condition.

Some individual players now make more money in one year than the combined salaries of the entire league of past generations.

There's no question that the game has changed. And in some respects, for the better.

But that 15- to 18-year period after the war produced the sharpest overall execution of pure baseball skills than anyone has ever seen since they started playing the game professionally.

I can't back up my belief with a book full of numbers and statistics. I was there, though; I witnessed it first hand. I played with and against some of these giants. Either as a player or a broadcaster,

I've been blessed with having been part of more than five decades in the game.

Individual players today are as good as or maybe even better than their predecessors of decades long ago. For overall brilliance, though, I don't believe there was a period when the game was played better overall than in those 15 to 18 years after the war.

It's impossible even to try to comment on all of the individual stars of that era. Besides, it wasn't merely the presence of those stars that made the period so great. It was the overall sharpness and crispness of play that constituted the brilliance of the era.

There's no question that players made errors. A lot of good hitters had to walk back to their dugouts after striking out with runners on base in key situations, too. Players weren't perfect. They made plenty of mistakes. On occasion they threw to the wrong base. Some failed to run out ground balls and others just kept on running until they scored or were tagged out.

Mistakes and failure always have been and always will be part of the game. If it weren't for some of the bad plays, we wouldn't appreciate the good ones as much as we do.

Overall, though, I think the quality of play was never brighter than it was back then.

It was a time when the execution of plays was done with the precision of a scalpel. Bunting ... the hit-and-run ... hitting behind a runner ... choking up on the bat with two strikes ... looking for a certain pitch ... knowing when to swing away and when to take a pitch ... hitting the cut-off man ... knowing when to try for the runner and when to use the relay.

Never in history has the game been played more fundamentally sound than it was in that period. There was no room for grandstanding. Players who tried it usually didn't stick around too long.

The same fundamentals remain very much part of the game today. It just seems that we don't see them practiced as regularly as we did in that Golden Era.

As I said, it's impossible to compare any other hitter with Ted Williams. It's simply not fair to Williams or the other hitter. Williams was that much better than everybody else. I played with Williams and I played against him. Every player looks better when you play against them. You fear a player more.

Williams was an exception to the rule. Playing with him every day, I got the opportunity to witness the genius of his talent. He had the most beautiful swing that God ever gave one man. Every time he went to the plate he put on a clinic for hitting.

He was always thinking hitting. He knew exactly what a pitcher was going to throw in every situation. He was never intimidated. He was always the intimidator.

Even after he made an out, he'd come back to the bench convinced there was no way in the world that pitcher could get him a second time.

"I've got him figured out now," he'd say. "I know exactly what he's going to throw me on every count. Let's go. Get me back up there." And usually Ted was right. He did have the pitcher figured out.

Playing with Williams made you glad he was on your side. No matter how far down you may have been in a game, you always had the feeling that Ted would come up with a couple of big hits to get you back into the game.

The amazing thing about Williams' career was that it was interrupted twice because of military service—once during World War II and then again during the Korean War. And this came during the prime of his career. I can't even imagine the numbers he would have put in the books had he been able to play his entire career.

Ted was an extremely patriotic person. He was a legitimate war hero. But he became very upset with the Marines after he was called back for the second time. He felt he already had served his time.

It's impossible even to speculate what kind of numbers Williams would have achieved had his career not been interrupted twice. One thing for sure, though, the numbers he would have posted would still be a target for young players today. It is impossible to list all the great players of that time. But I know there was no better hitter than Ted Williams. Not in that era or any other period of baseball history.

Except for exhibition games and All-Star Games, I didn't get much of an opportunity to see the National League players unless they were traded to our league.

No one can say for sure who the best all-around player was. That's one of the beauties of baseball. One person might pick Mickey Mantle and another might say Willie Mays. Someone might pick Joe DiMaggio and all three might be right.

For my personal pick, you don't have to look any further than center field in Yankee Stadium. There were two out there that deserve consideration. Either way you choose, you can't lose.

If it wasn't for all the injuries he suffered, Mickey Mantle could have been the greatest player that ever lived. For almost his entire career, though, he played as a cripple.

There wasn't one part of the game at which Mantle did not excel. He could hit the ball harder and farther than anyone. He hit for average. No one was faster. With all the hitters in the Yankee lineup, Mantle didn't have to steal bases or he might have set some records in that department. He could play center field easier than most men mow their front lawn. And he had an arm to back it up.

When Mantle was hot, he single-handedly destroyed a team. He could come into your town for a series and literally annihilate you with eight or nine hits. Because of that loaded Yankee lineup, it was difficult to pitch around him all the time.

And he did all of this with knees that had been sliced up like diced onions. There's no telling how good Mantle may have been had he been healthy his entire career.

Joe DiMaggio preceded Mantle in center field. For pure grace and style in every phase of the game, DiMaggio might have been the best.

DiMaggio never struck out with the tying or winning run on third base. That simply never happened. He never swung at a pitch in the dirt like you see some power hitters do. He always looked like he was in total control. There was no wasted effort. He was so smooth he almost looked mechanical.

Joe was the same way in center field. He was so graceful that it never looked like he was running hard. But he got to every ball and actually made the tough catches look routine. Joe looked like he never had to sweat; that's how easy he made the game look.

DiMaggio didn't have the raw power or blinding speed of Mickey Mantle. He just had a style and grace about him that baseball has never seen again.

Everybody always wanted to beat the Yankees because they always had the best ball players. We used to play them tough because we had pretty good pitching. We had Fred Hutchinson and Hal Newhouser and Art Houtteman and Dizzy Trout and Ted Gray. The Yankees didn't just come into town and hammer us. To beat us, they had to earn it.

But they never ran out of good players. When they needed somebody, they called him up from the farms with a snap of the fingers.

In 1950, for instance, we stuck with them all the way. Then in the middle of August, they turned to their minor league system and called up Whitey Ford.

All he did was come up and go 9-1. That was the difference. They beat us for the pennant by three games. They always had somebody to fill in any hole that developed.

Ford was definitely a key part of that Golden Era. He was a tough pitcher. He feared no hitter and no situation.

After facing him a few times, I knew exactly how he was going to pitch me. With Ford, it was real important to get him before he got two strikes on you.

He'd start me with a curve that would just barely miss or nick the outside corner. Then he'd throw me a fastball out there. Once he got two strikes on you, you were going to get a hard curve breaking down and in. Today you see some batters miss that pitch by a foot. Most of the time I knew it was coming and I still didn't get good wood on it.

He was so sharp with his pitches that most of the time it didn't matter if I knew what was coming. I did cross him up one time when he made a mistake trying to walk me. A couple of years ago, we were both in Phoenix and he laughed about the situation.

"The scored was tied in the ninth," he recalled. "There was a runner on second and you were up. Casey (Stengel) told me to walk you."

Ford got the first pitch a little too close to the plate. I reached over and lined it to right but it sliced just foul. Casey went to the mound to talk to Ford and Yogi Berra.

"If that S.O.B. wants to hit, then pitch to him," Casey told Ford.

I knew he was going to come in tight with a fastball on me. I sat on that pitch and ripped a base hit to left field to win the game. I knew that pitch was coming. I didn't want to make one mistake against Whitey. If he got you down in the count, he had you. He always had command of what he was doing. He never walked a batter when it meant something. Whitey Ford was one of the toughest competitors of any period. He belonged in that Golden Era.

Bob Feller was absolutely the toughest pitcher I ever faced. He threw the hardest. It wasn't just his speed, though. He had an idea of what he wanted to do. Then he'd let that fastball do all the talking.

Feller came back from the war at the end of the 1945 season. In 1946, he might have had his best season; he led the league with twenty-six wins and also set the all-time record of 348 strikeouts.

The Indians finished the season in Detroit that year. Feller pitched on Friday night and struck out his usual dozen. He was one strikeout shy of tying the all-time season mark.

Lou Boudreau announced Feller would start on Sunday with one day's rest. He was going to face Hal Newhouser. The two of them had a great rivalry going regarding who was the best pitcher in the league.

Before the game, we all laughed that none of us were going to be the record-tying victim for Feller.

The first eight hitters up at least got a piece of the ball. Then it got to Newhouser. He struck out and we did not let him forget it. Feller went on to strike out a few more to set the record.

That whole Cleveland staff was awesome. In fact, that probably was the best overall staff any team ever had. Bob Feller ... Bob Lemon ... Early Wynn ... Mike Garcia ... Herb Score. Then there were Don Mossi and Ray Narleski waiting for you in the bullpen.

There were plenty of outstanding pitchers in those days, but if I had to pick the next toughest after Feller, it probably was Lemon.

When we went into Cleveland for a four-game series, I used to lay there in bed before the start of the series and try to figure out how I could get a hit my first time up. If I could do that, I knew I couldn't go hitless for the weekend. That helped to take off some pressure.

I used to tell myself "maybe I'll bunt or try to hit-and-run ... anything not to strike out."

Against all those good pitchers, I drew a mental diagram of where to look for a certain pitch. If he painted the outside corner, I knew I couldn't hit it anyway. If I got that one pitch I was looking for, though, I'd jump on it.

If you went up to the plate with no idea of what to look for against those pitchers, you didn't have a chance. You might just as well have stayed in the dugout because it didn't matter.

Year in and year out in those golden days, the Yankees had the best teams. For that one season of 1954, though, I never witnessed a better single team than the Cleveland Indians. For just one year, they have to be ranked up with the best teams in history.

There are a lot of reasons why those nearly two decades after the war were the Golden Years.

• *All the veterans and all of the promising young players had returned from military service.* This had an immediate impact on the quality of play. The stars knew they had lost time in the primes of their careers. They were anxious to make up for lost time before they began to slow down. The promising young players had to compete against the stars and a lot of new young talent that had stepped in while they were gone. The competition was fierce.

• *Black players were allowed to compete in the major leagues.* Finally after decades of discrimination, the doors were opened to black players. After Jackie Robinson broke the color line, major league teams began to sign the star players of the old Negro Leagues. Some of the players in those leagues were better than we had in the majors. Again, this led to keen competition and a far better overall product.

• *Latin players were more actively pursued.* There had been some Latin players in the league already, but baseball seemed to step up its efforts to recruit more of the Latin stars. This put even more pressure on the traditional white players who suddenly found two and three players competing for their positions.

• *There were only 16 major league teams at the time.* Sheer numbers tell you that competition has to be tougher with only 16 major league teams compared to today's 30. Unless a player was a legitimate superstar, every year in spring training there were three or four candidates fighting for his job. Without diminishing the talents of the modern game, there are a lot of players in the major leagues today who never would have made it past Triple-A in those years.

• *Only two teams made it to post-season play.* In those days, there were no playoffs. There was one champion from the American League and one from the National.

I enjoy today's postseason format. With as many major league teams as there are, it's necessary to have some sort of elimination before the World Series.

When only two made it to October, though, every team had to stay sharp for the whole season. Even those who were eliminated from pennant contention could pick up some extra money by finishing in the first division.

• *The major league salary structure had not rocketed out of control.* I believe today's salary structure has had an impact on the quality of play. It takes a very special kind of player to perform to the best of his ability day in and day out with a contract that guarantees him several million dollars a year regardless of how he plays. That's simply human nature.

I'm afraid that today's huge salaries have taken some of the hunger out of the players. It's not all their fault. The owners are responsible for paying them. But the situation has played a part in weakening the quality of play.

•*The minor leagues were loaded with an abundance of teams.* Again, sheer numbers guaranteed that competition had to be strong. Each major league team had about ten or twelve minor league affiliates. Every spring a player had a couple of kids who had risen through the system and were competing for his job. A player couldn't afford to slack off or even have a prolonged slump. There was always someone there ready to take his place.

• *In big cities and small towns across the country, more kids were playing baseball.* I don't have any specific statistics. It simply seems like kids, in those days, played more baseball than anything else. There were pick-up games on the fields, in the streets and in the alleys.

Today there are so many more sports and other types of activities that compete for a youngster's time. Unless a youngster is playing in an organized league, it doesn't seem as though there are as many kids playing in the sandlots as there used to be.

• *Baseball used to stand as the unchallenged champion of all sports.* I think we have to be honest and admit that baseball no longer can stand alone and proclaim that it dominates sports the way it once did.

There was that time when every young boy dreamed about growing up and becoming a major league star. Sports like football and basketball were always big in the high schools and colleges. When it came to the pros, though, baseball sort of sat on a pedestal by itself.

Today baseball has lost a lot of good young athletes to other sports; not only to football and basketball, but also to golf and tennis. There's a lot more money in all sports today. The good young athlete has a wider career choice if he chooses professional athletics.

That's also reflected in today's media coverage. There was a time when baseball simply dominated all the sports pages and radio broadcasts. Television today has helped to lift all kinds of sports into widespread public awareness. Baseball has to compete for TV time and newspaper space more than ever before.

There have been many changes in the modern game of base-ball. To a degree, it can be argued that the quality of play has been diluted more than any other major sport. Nevertheless, I still love it and wouldn't trade one good ball game for a whole season of any other sport.

There was a time, though, that baseball ruled as undisputed champion of all sports. It was a beautiful time when I believe the game was played at its overall highest level.

It was the Golden Era of the game. I'm proud I played a little part in that history.

CHAPTER THIRTEEN

ALMOST IN THE DUGOUT

Almost every player who sticks around the big leagues for any length of time probably gets an itch to manage. I did. I also got the opportunity. And I'm glad I never took the job.

When I was a player, I thought I would make a good manager. When I played for the Tigers, I used to talk to Red Rolfe, the manager, about it all the time.

"When you were playing and the Yankees were winning all those pennants, did you ever think about managing?" I asked him.

"All the time," he said. "I wanted to manage the Yankees, but there wasn't much of a chance with Joe McCarthy there."

I told Red that I'd like to manage once my playing career was over.

"You should," he said. "You'd make a good manager."

I got the chance with the Tigers after the 1966 season. I could have had that 1968 championship team, but I have no regrets. By that time I was very satisfied with my broadcasting career and the fact that I was able to spend more time at home with my family.

In 1966, the Tigers were steadily moving toward a championship, but it was a catastrophic season with the deaths of two managers—Charlie Dressen and Bob Swift—in the same year.

We finished the season with a weekend series in Minnesota. Jim Campbell (Tiger general manager) and Rick Ferrell (assistant) joined us for the last three games.

At dinner after the game, we talked about the misfortune of the season and how those two deaths affected the team all year. When we returned to the hotel, Jim called me to his room.

"We've got to make some big changes and we want you to manage the club," Jim said.

I was stunned. Then I think I shocked him when I told him I was honored but I didn't want the job. I was very happy handling the television broadcasts.

"Mr. Fetzer [Tigers owner] wants you to manage and I want you to manage," he persisted. "You're the man we decided on."

I was still somewhat knocked off balance.

"Jim, you don't want a man who doesn't really want to manage your club," I reasoned. "I want to broadcast for the rest of my career. Besides, we're such good friends. In four or five years, you'll eventually have to fire me. That's what happens to managers. I don't want to put either of us in that position."

Jim didn't like my answer, but he knew I wasn't going to change my mind.

"Then you'll have to tell Mr. Fetzer," he said.

He called Mr. Fetzer immediately.

"I appreciate the confidence you have in me, but I'm a broadcaster now and I love it," I told Mr. Fetzer. "I feel very comfortable and I enjoy the time with my family."

If Mr. Fetzer had said either manage or you're fired, I would have thanked him and simply have gone home.

"I'd like to have you manage," Mr. Fetzer said. "I think you can handle the club. But if you feel so strongly about it, I perfectly understand."

If I really wanted to manage, I would have seized that opportunity in a second. The Tigers were a great young club just a blink away from making a run at a world championship. They had a good team in 1966. But there was too much confusion with two managers dying in the same year. No team can play over that kind of turmoil.

Even after the Tigers won in 1968, I never second-guessed myself for turning down the job. I wouldn't have taken any club, not even the Yankees. I was happy right where I was.

When I refused, a string of phone calls ended with the hiring of Mayo Smith a few days later.

Jim had admired Ralph Houk for many years. He was the first person Jim called. Jim eventually hired him a few years later, but he would have taken Houk right then. Houk was managing the Yankees at the time.

"Well, if you can't do it, can you recommend anyone?" he asked Houk.

Houk suggested Mayo Smith.

"He's a roving scout," Houk told him. "He's a good baseball man and I wouldn't be afraid to turn my club over to him."

Jim eventually reached Smith and the deal was completed quickly. Two years later, Smith was the manager of the world champions.

I studied managers my whole life. I started when I was a player and continued right on through my broadcasting career. Without a doubt, Sparky Anderson was the best manager I ever was associated with. He not only was a great manager, he was such a gentleman. He did so much good for the Detroit community. He created his charity that helps so many underprivileged children in Detroit.

There's not a person who Sparky touched that wasn't left with a lasting good impression. Sparky doesn't talk religion. He lives a good Christian life.

Whenever I'm asked to give a speech, people always ask me about Sparky. I tell them that he's just as good a person as he is a manager. And, in my opinion, there was no better manager.

There wasn't one player who didn't learn from Sparky and didn't admire him. They learned about baseball and learned about life. He cared about how his players performed on the field, and more importantly, he cared about how they learned to conduct themselves as human beings.

One year, the Tigers traded for a young infielder. He was as good a hitter as you'd want to see. He had great talent, but wound up playing for several clubs because he always was hurt.

When Campbell had the chance to get this young man, he asked Sparky if he wanted him. Sparky told Jim he could handle him. Sparky really believed this youngster could help.

This young man wound up doing the same thing at Detroit that he had done wherever he had played. He played a couple of days and then was out a couple.

That tore Sparky up because he realized how much talent the player actually possessed. Finally Sparky told Jim that this fellow would have to go. It hurt Sparky, but he tried to help that young man even under tough circumstances.

"Young man, you robbed yourself," Sparky told him. "You robbed yourself and your family out of a lot of money. You're making $400,000 a year and you don't want to play. You want to sit on the bench and draw your pay. Well, it don't work like that. I vouched for you when you came here. You're the only player I ever gave up on."

If a player couldn't play for Sparky, he couldn't play for anybody. I don't know of one player who didn't admire Sparky. Before you knew it, that young man was out of baseball.

Sparky was a great manager, he knew how to handle people. He won in both leagues. Like Casey used to say, "you could look it up." Sparky was fearless. Right or wrong, he made a decision and stuck with it regardless of the consequences.

I mentioned to him that I once thought about managing in the big leagues. I told him I wondered if I could have handled the pitchers.

"If I go to take a pitcher out and he tries to talk me out of it, what do I do?" I asked him once.

Just as he made all decisions, Sparky was quick and emphatic.

"If you let the pitcher talk you out of it, you got no business being a manager," he said. "When you leave that dugout, you've made up your mind already. I don't care if Cy Young is out there on the mound . . . he's coming out of the ball game."

Sparky squeezed more out of some clubs he had in Detroit than any human being had a right to do. He could get water out of a stone.

He had two or three clubs that had no business being in a pennant race. Somehow, though, Sparky kept them hanging around second or third place all summer. He made it look as if the club could just get hot for a couple of weeks, it could win the whole thing. And some of those clubs had no business being out of the second division.

When he first joined the Tigers, Sparky took the losses so hard. Too hard for his own good, I thought.

Jim Campbell, Al Kaline and I would go out to eat with him almost every night after we did the broadcasts. When he first came to Detroit, he took every defeat like he had lost his last dime. I've seen managers and players who took losses hard. Sparky actually looked like he was going to die.

There was one night in Baltimore when we were in the race. We had gone into the ninth inning with a two-run lead.

Suddenly Brooks Robinson hit a home run. Someone else reached base safely and then Frank Robinson connected for a homer to win the game.

After the game, we went to the Pimlico Race Track Hotel for dinner. All of us were upset with the loss. But Sparky just sat there and stared at his meal the whole night. He didn't take two bites.

I don't show my emotions outwardly too much. I couldn't contain them, though, when Sparky managed his last game for the Tigers in Baltimore on the last day of the 1995 season.

Kaline and I wanted to say good-bye to Sparky after the game. By the time we got down to the manager's office, it was packed with all of the writers and reporters and cameramen.

We stood outside of his office waiting for it to clear. Suddenly he spotted us and called us in. Sparky put his arms around both of us and I began to cry. I thought of all the good times this man had brought to Detroit and all the good he had done for the city. Sparky bled for the Tigers. He is one of the finest human beings I ever had the privilege to meet in my lifetime.

Ralph Houk did an outstanding job for the Tigers. And he never received the appreciation he deserved. Ralph came to the Tigers with the cards stacked against him. But he did the job with dignity and laid the foundation for an eventual championship.

"You can't win with this ball club," Campbell told Houk when he brought him to Detroit. "We're going through a transition. We're going to be all right down the road, but you've got a thankless job for now."

At the time, the Tigers were dismantling their championship team. It had gotten old and the Tigers were replacing all their fan favorites with young players from their farm system. There were guys like Lance Parrish and Alan Trammell and Lou Whitaker. But it was going to take time. And a whole lot of patience.

Houk had the stature to buy that time. He had the respect of all his players and everyone in the front office. Ralph Houk wasn't afraid to make a move. He wasn't afraid to fail. If a man is afraid to fail, I guarantee you he's going to fail a lot.

If Houk made a move that backfired, he wasn't afraid to try it the very next day if he thought it was right. He had great confidence in his ability. I have a tremendous amount of respect for him. He did a tremendous job of bridging the gap between Billy Martin and Sparky.

Billy was an outstanding field manager. The problem was that Billy could never manage himself. He couldn't handle his personal life.

He socialized with the players. He drank with the players. Sooner or later that's going to lead to trouble. It did for Billy and the whole Tiger organization.

I admired Billy's ability to run a game on the field. When a game started, he ran a game as well as anybody you'll see. He wasn't afraid of anyone or any situation. When he made a decision, it was the right decision. It might have been wrong, but he believed it was right and he refused to back down. That's the sign of a good manager. There was no indecision with Billy. There never was an in-between. His problems came off the field. He lived as hard there as he managed on the field.

As a player, I was blessed with the privilege of having played under Mr. Connie Mack. By the time I made it to the major leagues with the Athletics, Mr. Mack already was at the end of his career. He wasn't a good manager then, but I didn't expect him to be.

Just having the opportunity to play under him was good enough for me. In his own way, he's as much a legend in baseball as Babe Ruth or Mickey Mantle.

Red Rolfe might have been the best bench manager I ever played for. He ran the game better than anyone when I played. There wasn't a tiny thing about the game that he didn't notice. He was always two or three hitters ahead of everybody else at all times.

A lot of people felt Paul Richards was better at running a game. I played for Paul and we became very close friends. He stayed ahead of everyone because he was the type of manager who put the fear of God into every player.

I think for pure baseball strategy, though, Rolfe was the best that I played for. Rolfe's problem was that he had trouble getting along with his players. Hoot Evers hated him and Rolfe hated Hoot in return.

There was a time when we were a run down with no one out and a runner on second base in the ninth inning. Bob Swift was the batter and he grounded out weakly to third base without moving the runner up.

"No wonder you can't play," Rolfe shouted at Swift when he returned to the dugout. "You can't even hit the ball to right field when we have to move up a runner."

Swift got just as angry.

"That's the problem," Swift shouted back. "I've hit too many to right trying to help this team out."

Relations between Rolfe and the players always seemed strained. Sometimes he'd say a lot of things in the clubhouse that never should have been said.

Steve O'Neill was my first manager at Detroit. He was a kindly old gentleman who got fairly hot-headed. He was never afraid to tangle with umpires or even his own players. He wasn't the best manager I played for, but he was always into the game.

When I was traded to the Red Sox, Lou Boudreau was the manager. What impressed me most about Boudreau was the confidence he showed in himself. He wasn't worried about impressing anyone and it was tough to impress him.

He was totally secure in his own abilities. He had Bill McKechnie and Earl Combs as coaches. These were two giants in their own right.

A lot of managers might be intimidated by having such distinguished coaches. They might fear for their jobs. Not Boudreau. Lou knew where he stood with his coaches, his players, the front office and—most of all—with himself.

I watched Boudreau stand right next to McKechnie and ask for advice several times. I'd listen and try to learn because these were two great baseball minds.

When I was traded to the White Sox, Paul Richards was the manager. I was with him the rest of the way because we both went to the Orioles at about the same time. Paul was sharp as a whip. He let everybody know that he was the boss. He wasn't afraid of anyone and challenged everybody.

There wasn't a manager I played for or watched as a broadcaster who I didn't learn something from. I believe I would have enjoyed managing because I love the game so much.

But I can't say that I'm disappointed I never managed. I had too much fun broadcasting the games and being able to sleep at night once they were over.

CHAPTER FOURTEEN

IT WAS JUST TIME

When I was traded from Philadelphia to Detroit, I felt shocked more than anything else. When the Tigers sent me to Boston, I was confused.

It was a totally different feeling in 1954 when the Red Sox traded me to the White Sox.

More than anything else, I felt like I was being used.

I enjoyed Chicago. I always liked the city and I respected the organization. By that time, though, I felt like I was something of a pawn. It seemed like I was always the guy somebody had to have to get them to the top. The problem was that I always had to up-root my family as part of the deal.

I have to admit I felt a little disgusted.

I had hit .300 for eight years in a row. I made the All-Star team every year. But I always had to move. I was made keenly aware that baseball is a big business.

Joe Cronin was the general manager at Boston. He and I had become good friends. He was always honest and up front with me. In spring training of 1954 he told me that he might have to trade me.

"We don't want to trade you," he said. "But Frank Lane over at the White Sox thinks he's only a third baseman away from winning a pennant. He's made some very good offers for you. So far we've turned everything down. But I'm not going to say that we won't trade you."

On May 23 of that season, he did.

The Red Sox received Grady Hatton, another third baseman, and $125,000 in cash. That was a lot of money in those days.

I remember reading what Tom Yawkey (Red Sox owner) said in the paper.

"I hate to trade Kell," he said. "But it's time I got some money back. I've spent a lot of money on acquiring ball players and it's time I got some money back in return."

Paul Richards was managing the White Sox. We had played together on the Tigers and he was a good friend. I still didn't like having to pack up and start all over again, though.

I wound up having a bad year and batted only .283 for the White Sox. I bounced back in 1955 and led the team with a .312 average and 81 runs batted in.

But that trade took something out of me. I had lost something. That deal got me to thinking about retiring. It was a combination of things that had been growing over the years. More than anything, I felt guilty for having been away from home for so many years. My kids were growing up. In a few years my son was going to graduate from high school.

I had always felt guilty about being away from home so much. Early in my career, I thought I was some kind of bad person and was the only one who felt that way. Then I began to understand that at some point, almost every professional athlete begins to feel guilty.

By that time, though, that feeling really started to affect me. I thought about it all the time.

Charlene had to make so many sacrifices. She had to play both mother and father to our two kids when I was gone. She did a marvelous job, and she never complained once about all the hardships she had to face alone.

Once a season started, she'd stay in Swifton till the kids were out of school. Then she'd pack up our belongings and bring them to Detroit or Boston or Chicago where the family would spend the summer.

There had to be so many nights when they felt alone. Maybe there had been a storm and they were down in that big old house in Swifton waiting for it to pass while I was off in some city a thousand miles away. Maybe there had been some father-son banquet or a father-daughter get-together that my kids had to miss because I wasn't at home.

After young George had started to play baseball himself, I never could be around to watch his games. That's when I really understood how much my father had sacrificed for me. He never would miss one of my games. It didn't matter if he was sick or he had to miss work. He was as sure to be sitting in those stands as those mosquitoes back in Swifton were going to buzz around all summer.

I understood that I was only doing my job. I was providing for my family the best way I knew how with the gifts that God had given me. Charlene was my biggest source of encouragement. She knew I was a ball player. She understood the sacrifices it took. She knew what it all meant to the family. As the years rolled on, though, I began to feel more and more guilty.

After dinner following a ball game, I generally went back to my hotel room and read a book. It kept me busy. But those thoughts of always being away from home kept creeping into my mind like the lyrics of a song I couldn't forget.

All of those guilt feelings really started to mushroom once I was traded to Chicago. It wasn't because of the city. I had always liked Chicago. And I had always played fairly well in Comiskey Park.

It wasn't because of the White Sox, because I enjoyed all my teammates and we had a fairly good club. We won 91 games and finished third in both 1954 and 1955.

It was simply those doggone feelings of guilt that had been boiling inside my belly for so many years. They started to wear on me like a dull headache that refuses to go away. I believe that was the first time I seriously started to think about leaving the game and going back to Swifton full time. More than ever before, that's where I felt I should be.

When I was young, I had invested some money in farm land in Swifton. I farmed during the off-seasons. Eventually I knew that I would become more active in it.

Charlene and I never had expensive tastes. We lived quite modestly and had saved some money. I was seriously tempted to call it quits right then and go back home and make a living off the land that we owned.

As usual, though, Charlene had thought the whole situation through quite thoroughly. She understood the loneliness I was feeling. She would have supported me regardless of my decision.

But she reasoned with me. She explained that if I were to quit at such a young age, I might have regrets over it for the rest of my life. She helped me to understand that I was a ball player. God had blessed me with some very special gifts and I still had some good playing time left in me. She didn't think I should waste the opportunity. She knew I wasn't away from home deliberately. It was my job. I was trying to provide for my family the best way I could.

Charlene was right. I knew I had to kick myself back onto the right track. In 1955 I had a good year. My confidence was solid and I could see that it wouldn't be all that long before we were all back in Swifton for good.

At the end of the 1955 season, Paul Richards received a fantastic offer from Baltimore. The franchise was new to Baltimore in 1954. It was the old St. Louis Browns.

Richards went to the Orioles as manager and general manager. He had total control of the entire franchise. One of the first moves he made was to get me over there.

"I'll get you here," he told me. "The only thing the club has to offer right now is me and you."

I was flattered, but in good conscience, I told Paul that I wasn't going to play much longer.

Nevertheless, on May 21, 1956, the Orioles traded Dave Philley and Jim Wilson for Bob Nieman, Mike Fornieles, Connie Johnson and me. Richards made the deal as quickly as he could. I played every day for the Orioles and batted .261.

After that season, though, I made up my mind I would play only one more year. I really didn't even feel like doing that, but the Orioles had made quite a commitment to get me. I figured I owed it to them.

When I finished that season, I had just turned 35 years old. I could have hung on for another three or four years. I always stayed in shape and I felt confident enough to know that I would not embarrass myself.

But I had talked it over with Charlene and the kids. They were tickled to death that 1957 was going to be my final season. Nothing in the world could have changed my mind.

With my mind back on the game and knowing that was my final season, I played pretty well. I was determined to hit .300 if it was at all possible. I fell just a couple of hits shy and finished at .297. I only made four errors. Overall, it was a pretty good year.

Before the season ended I told Richards that I was going to retire. Somehow he didn't believe me. He felt sure he could convince me to come back for at least one more season.

In January, Richards sent me a contract for the 1958 season just as if it was my first year. I mailed it back and told him that I would not return under any circumstances.

A few weeks passed and he called me in Swifton.

"I talked to the owners and they told me to offer you a little more money," Richards said.

I was making the same $45,500 a season that I started earning in Detroit.

"It's not a matter of money," I told him. "You could offer me a whole lot more and it wouldn't make a lick of difference. It's just time. I told you last season I already had talked to my family and we all decided it was time for me to leave."

Another week passed before he called me again. He said he was going to fly into Memphis. He asked if I would meet him at the Peabody Hotel. Out of courtesy to a friend, I agreed to meet him. But my mind was made up. My decision was final.

George, Jr. was going to graduate from high school in a couple of months. Terrie was in the ninth grade. If there was even the slightest possibility of changing my mind, it was eliminated at the breakfast table the morning I was going to Memphis.

"Daddy, I wish you wouldn't go over there to talk to that old Paul Richards," Terrie said. "He'll talk you into playing and you said you were going to quit."

Now how could I have played after that?

"Honey, I'm not going to play ball," I told her. "I made you a promise and that's it."

Richards and I talked for two hours in the Peabody. Paul was an up front guy and tried to persuade me into one more year. After giving me his best sales pitch, he finally was convinced that I would not change my mind.

"You're not going to play ball," he said. "I could hit you in the head and you still wouldn't play. I can see that."

Finally we agreed on something.

"No, Paul," I said. "My playing career is over."

As general manager of the Orioles, Paul was disappointed. As a long-time friend, though, he was happy with my decision.

"What are you going to do?" he asked.

I told him that as a young player, I had invested money in some farm land in Swifton. I used to farm a little during the off-seasons and now I was going to try it full time. I really had no other opportunities.

"Would you take a job on the weekends where you'd just be away from home on Saturdays and Sundays?" he asked.

I told him I'd love it, but I didn't think anyone would want to give me something like that.

Richards told me he had been contacted by CBS-Television. The network was looking for someone to work with Dizzy Dean and Buddy Blattner on the Game of the Week. It was a minor role, but CBS wanted a third man to open the show and do an interview.

"They called to ask me if I could recommend a former player," Richards said. "I told them I knew one player who could do a fine job for them, but I was going to try to talk him into playing one more year. It looks to me now, though, that you've just become a former player."

I thanked him for the recommendation. I returned to Swifton and called CBS President Bill MacPhail the next morning.

MacPhail asked me to come to New York, at the network's expense, to conduct an interview. I was put into a room with a complete stranger and instructed to interview him as if he were the star of a baseball team.

After that was finished, they asked me to interview another fellow as if he were the starting pitcher of an important game. When the interviews were completed, they thanked me and I returned to Swifton.

"We won't hear any more from them," I told Charlene when I got home. "I am now officially a farmer in Swifton."

Three days later I received a call from MacPhail. He offered me the job and I accepted as quickly as I could get the words out of my mouth.

Our first telecast was going to be from spring training. He sent me a schedule and told me to prepare myself.

The rest is history. I felt just like that kid again who had been signed by Mr. Mack 15 years earlier.

CHAPTER FIFTEEN
_____

BEHIND THE MIKE AND TALKING TO CASEY

M y venture into the world of baseball broadcasting was so sudden that I really didn't have time to worry about anything. There was no time to get scared. Everything happened too fast.

When I was a player, I was always cooperative with all the members of the media because I thought that was just the way any good person was supposed to act. The writers and broadcasters had a job to do just as I did. I always figured they were helping my career move along, too.

As long as they were fair and honest, I didn't have any problems with what they wrote or reported over the air. If I had made an error or a mistake in a game, then I expected them to point it out. If they didn't, then they weren't performing their jobs the way they were supposed to.

In turn, I believe most members of the media enjoyed dealing with me as a player. I think they recognized that I cooperated with them. I wasn't very colorful, but I always gave them honest answers. I always treated them with respect.

Of course, the media was different in those days. Back then, there weren't as many people covering games and coming out to the park as there are today.

Each newspaper had a regular beat writer who covered each game at home and on the road. If we played a game, that writer was there. When I played for Detroit, the city had three major daily newspapers—*The Detroit News, The Detroit Free Press* and *The Detroit Times*. All three were excellent papers and each one had a good baseball beat writer who traveled with us wherever we went.

In those days, the sports columnist for each paper also spent a lot of time at the park. Baseball was always the lead sports story. It's a little different today with so many sports competing for news space and air time.

Because this was the normal mode of operation at almost every major paper in the country, players at least recognized the writers for the other teams even if we didn't know their names.

Today there are so many different writers at each game that it's hard to get to know all of them. They seem to come from all departments of the newspapers, not just sports. There also are a lot more sports magazines or, at least, magazines that want feature stories on different athletes.

It's the same thing with radio and television stations. It's not just the stations' sports reporters who come to the park looking for stories. They come from the news and the feature departments. Sometimes even the weather people do their reports from the park.

The focus of a lot of sports reporting today also has changed. It used to be that the writers focused pretty much on what happened in the games. Today the focus has expanded to salaries, labor and all other kinds of things. A player's life gets fairly well dissected from the kind of cereal he eats for breakfast to the type of movies he enjoys.

That can be good and bad. It's good that a player can generate an inordinate amount of publicity that has nothing to do with what he's doing on the field. It can help build a player's image and make him a lot of money through endorsements and a variety of business opportunities.

It can be bad, though, for a player's personal life if he's not careful. Ball players today are almost treated like politicians. Every move they make is subject to some kind of scrutiny by the media. Even if I were playing today, the switch in media coverage probably wouldn't affect me. I led what a lot of media members might call a dull life.

I played every game as hard as I could. If we were playing at home, when the game was over I'd go straight to my house and spend the rest of the day with my wife and children. If we were playing on the road, I'd go get dinner after the game and then return to my hotel room and lay around reading a book. That may sound dull to a lot of people, but I enjoyed every minute of it.

When I was a player, I never gave any thought to a broadcasting career, even though I did receive a little broadcast experience when I played in Detroit and Harry Heilmann handled the radio.

For three straight spring trainings, Harry and I did a radio talk show back to Detroit. People used to call in and ask questions about how the team was going to do and various other topics in baseball.

Harry carried the show. By that time, he had become a polished professional. He knew how to get the show going and how to keep it flowing. He knew how to bring me into that flow so that the fans got the opportunity to talk to a player who they were going to watch all summer long.

I never was fearful of doing the show. I felt safe because I knew Harry was going to carry the ball and it was on radio going back to the Detroit fans. I already had established a pretty good rapport with them.

Even then, I never gave one thought to making a career out of broadcasting. The offer from CBS was totally different than the work I had done with Harry. This was television and it was going to be seen nationwide.

At that time, television was in its infancy. It was an unknown to a lot of people. A good portion of the public didn't pay much attention to it.

Maybe I should have been scared, but I wasn't. I was conscious of my Arkansas accent. To a lot of viewers, I knew I might sound a little different. If nothing else, though, I knew I would be conscientious. That's why I felt comfortable with the fact that if I worked hard, I could handle the job.

Television was good for baseball. And I felt I knew enough about the game to do a good job. Even then, I never thought it would develop into a real career. I never had designs of pursuing a lifetime in it.

MacPhail told me they would pay me $15,000 a year plus all expenses. That was less than I made for playing baseball, but tremendous money for working only weekends.

Besides opening the telecast, my job was to conduct a ten- to twelve-minute pre-game interview with a player or manager from one of the two teams. Factoring in two or three commercials, all I really had to fill was about five minutes of air time.

Our first telecast featured the New York Yankees. I felt pretty good because I knew several players on the Yankees. They were easy interviews because they won all the time. People were interested in what they had to say.

"We want you to interview Casey Stengel," MacPhail said.

When he told me this, I have to admit that I did become a little concerned.

Casey Stengel, to me, was a legitimate baseball legend. He not only was the most successful manager in history, but he also was a bona fide celebrity. His fame actually transcended the game.

I might have shaken Casey's hand a few times. But I can't say that I actually knew him. I was afraid Casey wouldn't even have a clue of who I was. What if he never even realized that I had played against all of his great teams?

"Couldn't I maybe interview Phil Rizzuto or Mickey Mantle?" I asked MacPhail. "I played against those guys. I know them pretty well. I'd feel a lot more relaxed with someone like that."

MacPhail was a professional. He knew what he was doing. He knew that all the fans loved to hear Casey talk. It didn't matter what he said, Casey was always a story. There was no better way to start a season than with Casey Stengel. And MacPhail wasn't going to let the opportunity slip away.

"Let's do Casey," he said. "You'll do fine with him."

So Casey it was.

The game was played in Jacksonville, Florida. If I wasn't nervous before, I was scared to death that morning. I called Casey in his room to ask if he would do the interview.

"Come on over here now, son," Casey said. "Let's talk a little ahead of time."

Casey invited me to breakfast and I sat there listening to the great man tell story after story. I didn't want that breakfast to end.

"I'll tell you what I had in mind for the show," I told him. "You've got so many great hitters on your club. Hank Bauer hits 25 to 30 home runs a year and he's your leadoff man. I'd like to ask you why you lead off with Bauer and how you go about making out a lineup with so many good hitters on your team."

Casey said, "That's good. You ask me that and I'll tell you why."

By the time I got to the park, I felt a whole lot better than I had before I talked to Casey. When the show started, I asked Casey about Bauer just as we had planned.

"You ask me why I bat Bauer first and I'll tell you why," Casey started. "Bauer is the kind of guy who hits me doubles and triples and sometimes a home run. Now when he gets up there and hits me a double or a triple, I don't have to bunt him over. And..."

He went on and on and on. He went up and down his entire lineup. He told me a little something on every hitter and then some.

I saw the director giving me the "cut" sign. It was time for a commercial. Finally I was able to ease in between a couple of Casey's sentences to tell him we had to take a break.

When we came back from the commercial, I asked Casey just one more question. He was off again as if he had never stopped talking.

He told stories, mixed in a few jokes and had all of us so mesmerized that the show had come to an end before I even realized we had run out of time.

I thanked Casey for his time and wished him luck for the season. I had asked him only two questions. I didn't know if the show had gone well or if I had bombed bigger than striking out with the bases loaded in the ninth.

When I reached the booth for the start of the game, the director told me MacPhail wanted to talk to me from New York.

"That was great," he said. "Just great. It was exactly what I was looking for. You can talk to all these people. They'll tell you things they won't tell anyone else. That was tremendous."

Dizzy Dean had it written into his contract that he would get every fifth weekend off. That meant I got the chance to work the game with Buddy Blattner.

It was tremendous experience for a first-year broadcaster like me. I had a network job. I was working with a couple of pros like Dean and Blattner. I was making $15,000 a year. And the best part about the situation was that I was only gone on weekends. The rest of the time I was home with my family in Swifton.

Then just as suddenly as they had the previous off-season, things changed again.

Only this time even more drastically.

CHAPTER SIXTEEN

HELLO, DETROIT ... AGAIN

After the 1958 season, baseball was terribly shocked by the sudden death of Mel Ott in an awful automobile accident. Mel was a member of Baseball's Hall of Fame and had served as Van Patrick's partner on the Tiger broadcasts from 1956 through 1958.

Charlene and I were driving home from an Arkansas football game on Saturday afternoon when we heard the news on the radio.

"We're going to get a call from Detroit," I told Charlene. "The Tigers are going to be looking for an ex-player to do the broadcasts."

I don't know why I felt that the Tigers were going to call me. I only had one year of broadcast experience and I still wasn't sure why CBS had picked me in the first place. For some reason, though, I had a feeling that the Tigers were going to call.

Sure enough, when we got home, there was a message to call Harry Sisson in Detroit. Harry was the Tigers' business manager and a real fine gentleman.

The Tigers wanted me to come back to Detroit to work with Van Patrick as the No. 2 commentator for the 1959 season. At that time, the Tiger radio broadcasts were carried by Station WKMH. The television games were simulcast over Station WJBK-TV.

Of course, I was flattered. At the time, though, I was not prepared to leave the situation I had. I had a great job and did not want to return to baseball on a full-time basis.

"Mr. Sisson, you're talking about coming back and working every day," I told him. "I'm honored that you would even consider me. But I quit playing because I wanted to spend more time with my family in Swifton. I just can't do it."

Sisson understood, but he was persistent.

"Have you ever met Mr. Fetzer?" Sisson asked.

John Fetzer had put together the syndicate that had purchased the Tigers from the Briggs Estate in the middle of the 1956 season.

"Mr. Fetzer is a great admirer of yours," Sisson continued. "He's a tremendous supporter of the Tiger franchise. He's going to be a great owner and a great asset to the city. You owe it to him to come up here and at least talk with him. We'll send you a plane ticket. The two of you should at least meet."

I explained to Charlene what Sisson had said. She agreed with Sisson that I should at least meet Mr. Fetzer so that both of us could communicate face to face.

I had never met Mr. Fetzer before. I knew he was a very successful owner of radio and television stations. I also had heard he was an incurable baseball fan—particularly of the Tigers.

It's very difficult to describe Mr. Fetzer precisely. He was such an imposing figure in a very gentle and sensitive manner. He had such a commanding presence about him. When he walked into a room, even before he said anything, he radiated a feeling that he was in charge. He wasn't pushy. He was simply possessed with this magnificent gift of presence.

Of all the people I've had the privilege to meet in my baseball, broadcasting and business career, Mr. Fetzer was one of the most intelligent. He also was sincere. He was sincere with the people who worked for him and extremely sincere about his love for baseball and the Tigers.

I was so fortunate to have worked or played for three legendary owners like Mr. Connie Mack, Mr. Tom Yawkey and Mr. John Fetzer. It's not fair to say one was better than another. But I do believe that no one exercised more concern and devoted more time to the overall good of the game than did Mr. Fetzer.

He was a very special man. People don't realize how much he personally sacrificed for the good of baseball. That's just the way he was. I don't believe baseball will ever again see another owner like Mr. Fetzer.

Mr. Fetzer, Sisson and I were discussing the Tiger broadcasting vacancy. For whatever reason, Sisson discreetly left the room. At that point, Mr. Fetzer became very serious.

"We want you very much to come back to Detroit as one of our broadcasters," he said. "We'll pay you $20,000."

I think one of the reasons Mr. Fetzer wanted me was because he appreciated the fact that I was not just a "dumb ball player" going up into the booth to make cute and funny statements. He knew that I was a businessman. I owned farm land. I owned the Kell Motor Company back in Swifton. He respected that.

I explained that I could return to CBS for $15,000 and just work weekends.

"You name the figure then," he said.

I had convinced myself I wasn't going to return to Detroit so I threw out a ridiculous number.

"You've got it," he said quickly.

Before I left that room, I had signed a five-year contract to work all 154 Tiger games as the No. 2 broadcaster. To this day I can only speculate as to why I changed my mind and signed that contract. I'm really not certain.

One of the main reasons was the sincerity of Mr. Fetzer. I could tell immediately that he was genuinely concerned about the Detroit Tigers. He loved that franchise like he loved a son. He had made a commitment to himself to turn it into the finest franchise in professional sports.

If it had been any other franchise, I still would have refused. But I had fallen in love with the Tigers since the days when I played there. Even after I was traded, I never lost that love affair with the Tigers.

I loved the franchise and I loved the city. The fans had always been so good to me. Swifton will always be home, but I've always felt so comfortable in Detroit. For whatever reason, I walked out of that room as a member of the Tiger organization.

I went straight to my hotel room and called Charlene. That was one of the hardest phone calls I ever made in my life. As usual, though, Charlene was supportive.

"If that's what you want to do then we'll work it out," she said. "I'm glad it's with the Tigers and you're going to do an outstanding job."

I worked with Van Patrick and did the middle three innings for just the 1959 season. Stroh's Beer became the major sponsor of the broadcasts after that season. Because Van had been so closely identified with Goebel's Beer for so many years, Stroh's worked out a deal to replace him.

Sisson invited me to a meeting with Peter Stroh. At that meeting it was agreed that I would become a co-announcer instead of the No. 2 man. I was asked if there was someone I would like as a partner.

My first reaction was to get Curt Gowdy. He was doing the Red Sox games and I knew he wasn't about to leave Boston. I suggested Ernie Harwell. He was doing the Orioles games and I had gotten to know him a little when I was in Baltimore. They told me to call him and see if he was interested. Ernie agreed and we started the 1960 season as a team.

I had a great time at the beginning of that five-year deal. On the next to last day of the 1959 season, I received a call from Tom Gallery who was the president of CBS.

"George, it looks like the Dodgers and the Milwaukee Braves are going to wind up in a tie for first place," he said. "Would you be available to do the playoffs for us with Buddy Blattner? And then we'd like for you to do the World Series with Joe Garagiola."

I almost fell out of my chair. I was a first-year play-by-play man and I had just been asked to do the Playoffs and the World Series.

He said to keep an eye on the scoreboard during my Tiger broadcast. If the Dodgers and Braves finished tied for first, he wanted me in Milwaukee for a 7 a.m. Monday production meeting. The teams did finish in a tie, and I hopped a plane to Milwaukee as soon as the Tiger season was over.

I was excited about doing my first post-season broadcast. When I went to the coffee shop for breakfast, though, I got another shock—this one from Blattner.

"Partner, I may not be able to work with you today," he said.

At first I thought he was kidding. Then I realized it was no time for jokes.

"What do you mean?" I asked. "I'm still new to this. I need all the help I can get."

Blattner explained that Dizzy Dean was upset that he hadn't been chosen to work the Playoffs. He told Blattner that if he wasn't working, then Blattner wouldn't either. Dean was close to the people at Falstaff Brewery who were major sponsors and had enough influence to get his way.

Gallery was just as firm with his decision to have Blattner and me work as the Playoff broadcast team. About a half-hour before the first game, Gallery told me I was going to do the games by myself.

Network television, all across the country...and all by myself!

Blattner wound up quitting his association with Falstaff and Dean. He did not work the games, but he sat in the booth and gave me some help.

The Dodgers won the first game. We flew to Los Angeles and they won the second in 14 innings to make it to the World Series.

And I had done both Playoff games alone.

For the World Series between the Dodgers and White Sox, I did a pre-game interview show. When the Series was over, I couldn't believe the Cinderella season I enjoyed my first year in the Tigers' booth.

In 1960, Gallery asked me to do the All-Star Game in Chicago. Then in 1962, he asked me to do the World Series between the Yankees and the San Francisco Giants on radio.

Mel Allen was a broadcaster for the Yankees and Russ Hodges worked for the Giants. They handled television for the Series. Garagiola and I were assigned to radio.

Gallery told Joe and me to decide between ourselves who would handle the play-by-play and who would do color. Joe said he wanted to do color. That tickled me to death because I wanted the play-by-play. It was a dream because I handled all nine innings of play-by-play for seven games of the World Series.

It was a privilege to work with Garagiola. He was extremely knowledgeable. He never got rattled; he made everything run so smoothly and never missed a play. He was a lot like Tim McCarver, but, in my opinion, better.

I'm not sure why Gallery took such a liking to me.

"I just love that voice," he kept telling me. "And I love the way you handle a broadcast."

From a professional standpoint, I couldn't have asked for a better situation than I had in Detroit. The Tigers treated me extremely well. I was getting the opportunity to handle some national broadcasts. As always, the fans were very good to me. But that guilty feeling of being away from home so much jumped up and bit me like a rattlesnake.

Charlene understood the demands of my job. So did George, Jr. and Terrie. I was the one with the problem. I just couldn't shake that devil.

There was one night when Charlene called me in Detroit after midnight. By this time, the kids were getting older. George, Jr.

already was in high school. He and Terrie had friends in Swifton they didn't want to leave for the whole summer. Charlene was crying and I was about to panic.

She had gone upstairs to George, Jr.'s room and discovered he had slipped out the window. He went down to the river with a bunch of friends. I imagine they had a little party with beer as a lot of kids that age do.

I called Jim Campbell immediately. I told him I had an emergency at home and had to go back to Swifton. I caught a plane to Memphis early the next morning. By noon I was in Swifton. The Tigers were off the next day before starting a series in Chicago on Tuesday night.

I made it to Chicago in time for the broadcast. But first I had a long talk with my son. I explained to him that I had signed a five-year contract. Until it expired, I was obligated to honor it. I told him that while I was gone, he would have to "take care of the two ladies in the house."

George, Jr. was a good boy and we never had a problem after that. I never could forget that incident, though. I never was able to shake all those feelings of guilt. Terrie seemed to handle my being gone a little better. I know how hard it was on George, Jr.

At the end of August in 1963, I told Mr. Fetzer and Campbell that I would not return for the following season. I had fulfilled my contract. This time I was convinced I could not be away from my family from spring training through the end of the season any more.

At first, Mr. Fetzer didn't quite believe me.

"Is there some other reason that you wish to leave?" he asked. "Do you want more money? Do you have a problem working with Harwell?"

I explained that I had no complaints.

"Mr. Fetzer, this is the way it's got to be," I said. "I signed this five-year contract knowing down deep that I should be home and I honored it. Now it's time for me to be with my family in Swifton."

At that point, he realized I would not change my mind.

"George, we want you on the Tiger broadcasts," he said. "You spend next season at home and we'll still pay half of your salary. But we are going to work this out some way so that you're still part of the team and everyone is satisfied."

Mr. Fetzer kept his word. For the 1964 season, he brought in Bob Scheffing, the former Tiger manager, to work with Harwell. Mr. Fetzer had different plans for 1965.

"I've got it worked out," he told me over the telephone in November. "Now listen very carefully because here's the way you said you wanted it and here's the way it's going to be.

"I'm going to separate the television and radio teams. I'm going to put you in charge of television with a new partner. I'm going to put Harwell in charge of radio with a new partner.

"We're going to televise 45 games. You can arrive on the day of the game and leave for home right after the telecast. Just don't miss a game."

For me, it was the perfect situation. I was able to return to Detroit as part of the broadcast team and still spend most of my time with my family in Swifton where I was convinced I should be.

"I can handle that, Mr. Fetzer," I told him. "And I promise you I won't miss any games." There were a couple of close calls because of airplane connections over the years. But I kept that promise.

"Is everything all right?" Mr. Fetzer would ask me occasionally over the years.

"Everything is perfect," I said.

It truly was. I had the perfect situation for more years than I could ever hope for.

No broadcaster in baseball was ever treated better than I was in Detroit—my home away from Swifton.

CHAPTER SEVENTEEN

"HELLO EVERYBODY...I'M GEORGE KELL"

When I first started my broadcasting career with the Tigers, Mr. Fetzer gave me the best piece of advice.

"Just be yourself," he said. "Don't try to be something you are not because it will never work. The fans will see through that immediately. I hired you because you are George Kell and you have a gift for calling a game. Now just go out and be George Kell."

That sounds so simple, but I kept those words with me throughout my career. It doesn't matter what a person does in life, those are wise words for everyone to live by.

I treated that broadcast booth with the same respect I treated the field when I was a player. I had to work hard as a player to develop the gifts that God gave me. I took the same attitude to the booth. I promised myself to make every sacrifice and do whatever it took to become a respected baseball broadcaster.

There are a lot of young announcers who get the job simply because they were former ball players. I didn't want that. I wanted to become as professionally accomplished in the booth as I had been on the field.

I worked at it. I tried to improve myself all the time. I listened to other announcers. I think Jack Buck was one of the best in baseball broadcasting history. I never tried to copy another broadcaster's voice, phrases or style. I just studied how they handled different situations. I tried to determine for myself what distinguished the good ones from the rest of the pack.

A few years ago, I made a speech in Lansing, Michigan, for a bank I've represented for many years. There were a lot of young people in the audience.

"You mentioned about when you played for the Tigers," a young lady of about 30 said to me after the speech.

"I never knew you played ball yourself. I've enjoyed listening to you for as long as I've lived, but I never knew you actually played in the major leagues."

I was not offended by her remark. In fact, I took it as a compliment. If I was that good of an announcer that she accepted me for those skills and not just the fact that I was a former player, then I had to feel good.

I wanted people to accept me as a professional announcer. I didn't want them to think I got the job just because I used to play third base for the Tigers or because I happen to be in the Hall of Fame. I wanted people to know I was proud to be the voice of the Detroit Tigers.

I always stayed myself. I tried to keep my broadcasts as if I were talking to someone sitting in the same living as I was. I let the game unfold in front of me and just tried to accurately relate what was happening on the field.

I'm not a flashy guy, so I never tried to get too fancy with words or descriptions. If a player made a good play, I called it a good play. If it was a bad play, I called it a bad play. If a broadcaster tries to cover up what every viewer has seen with his own eyes, then that announcer's credibility is zero. If a ball club wants their man to do something like that, then they don't want a broadcaster. They want a cheerleader.

I changed my approach to calling a game several years ago. At the beginning, I didn't know that much about the profession. I had played for the Tigers. I had an undying love affair for the Tigers. I was such a fan, I admit that I had become a cheerleader. I didn't realize it until a few of my very close friends were honest and mentioned it to me.

"George, for the most part, everybody you are talking to during a broadcast are basically Tiger fans," they said. "They're just as much a fan as you are. It's all right for them to cheer. But you're a professional. You're paid by the Tigers to call the games. You're not paid to be a cheerleader."

That struck me square between the eyes. It made a lot of sense. From that day forward, I was very careful not to give any appearance of being a cheerleader.

Over the years I have listened to too many announcers that were so biased in favor of the home team that it became impossible for them to give a professionally accurate account of the game. I never did like that type of approach. I said to myself, if I'm sounding like that, then I have to do something about it.

And I did. In fact, maybe I went a step too far and became too low-keyed with my descriptions. But I must have been doing something right because in my 38 years in the broadcast booth, I didn't get but about five letters that criticized my approach.

I know one thing for sure. Jim Campbell was pleased with the way I handled the games. Even more important, so was Mr. Fetzer.

Mr. Fetzer did not want his broadcasters serving as "homers." Cheerleading is for football games on the sidelines. Mr. Fetzer wanted a straight line broadcast. He wanted it honest coupled with the insight I could provide from all my years of experience.

"I like the way you report the game," he told me once while we were traveling on a plane. "If a ball goes through the third baseman's legs, I like the way you say, 'He should have had it.'

"You don't criticize him or beat him up. But the man should have made the play. Everybody who was sitting in the park knows he should have made the play and the viewers should share in that feeling."

When an announcer is a homer, he insults the intelligence of every viewer and listener of the game. Baseball fans, especially Tiger fans, know the game. You can't fool them. They can see right through that little trick. They can tell right off the reel if you're a phony. They don't want a huckster, they want the truth.

There's no question I wanted the Tigers to do well. But wishing them well and leading cheers from the broadcast booth are two very different things.

I learned a lot about broadcasting from working with Ernie Harwell shortly after I took the job with the Tigers. He already had been in the business for several years and was a professional at the way he went about calling a game.

There was no nonsense with Ernie. He saw a play and called it as he saw it. If you twist the truth, you're only bending your own credibility. Once a broadcaster loses that, he might as well pack up and go home. I learned a lot of things from Ernie that I carried throughout the rest of my career.

I'm a little perturbed with some of the younger announcers who come into the business thinking that they know everything there is to know about the game. They haven't even taken time to pay their dues.

I love to watch ESPN. But that network is doing so many sports now that they're hiring people who do not have the proper background in sports reporting.

They may work for ESPN. They may be called professional sports broadcasters. But all they're doing is reading scripts in front of the camera. They try to be cute by telling stories about old-time players. But it's so easy to tell that all they're doing is reading lines that someone else has written.

I don't think it's wrong pulling for the home team within your heart. But what you put out over the air should be honest and straightforward. Let the viewer and the listener be the judge. You are not going to fool the real baseball fan.

Harry Carey is a homer. But that's Harry's act. He takes it past the limit of what's believable. The viewer knows it's all part of the show.

That's why if I had to pick just one favorite from all of the broadcasters I've either worked with or listened to, it would have to be Jack Buck. He was honest. He made his point. And he wasn't afraid to call the game the way it was played. He was a professional all the way.

During all the years I did the Tiger broadcasts I never was told what I could or could not say. Mr. Fetzer, in fact, believed very strongly that censorship like that would cripple a broadcaster. It would not be consistent with the integrity of the broadcast.

I know I made my share of mistakes over the years. When you are doing so many live telecasts, it's impossible not to stumble over some facts or even some of the action on the field.

Maybe it's because I try not to use foul language in my everyday speech, but I never let something slip out on the air that would have been embarrassing to me, my family, the Tigers or the station. The closest thing to something like that occurred during a Sunday afternoon telecast from Boston and I heard about it as soon as the inning ended.

Kirk Gibson was playing right field for the Tigers. I had just said it looked like there might be a rain delay soon when I looked up and saw some goofball run out onto the field and straight up to Gibson.

Gibson was never one to flinch from anyone. He just pushed the guy away. That guy bounced back and went right up to Gibson again and received another shove. This happened three or four times and not one security guard made a move to remove this guy from the field. He could have had a gun or knife or any kind of weapon.

"For chrissakes...is nobody gonna help Gibson?" I blurted into the microphone.

As soon as it had come out of my mouth, I realized what I had said. I went silent for a few seconds. It seemed like an eternity. In my mind, I kept asking myself what I had said. I knew it wasn't terrible, but it was not the sort of thing anyone is supposed to say on live television.

Joe Falls, a columnist for *The Detroit News,* was in the pressbox next to the broadcast booth. About ten minutes after I had made the statement, he came into the booth and asked if he could talk to me after the inning ended.

I knew immediately what had happened. Joe had received a call from someone at his paper back in Detroit. The paper was looking for a statement about what I had said.

"The paper called and wants me to ask you if you said 'chrissakes' over the air," Joe said.

"I did," I told him simply.

I think Joe was a little surprised by my quick admission. Maybe he thought I would deny it.

"The man could have stuck Gibson with a knife," I said.

Joe is a good reporter. He understands all the little nuances of a ball game.

"Can you live with what you said?" he asked.

"I have to," I answered. "I said it."

That's all he had to hear. He turned around, left the booth and never wrote a word about it.

After the game before we even left the park, I got a call from Jim Campbell.

"What's going on in Boston?" he said.

"We just got beat, that's what's going on," I answered.

I could tell he had called just to pull my leg.

"Someone just called me and said that you let out an oath over the air," he said.

"I don't think I let out an oath," I answered. "I just used a Jim Campbell saying that I hear so many times from him."

Campbell just about died laughing.

"Well, I'm not laughing," I said. "I said it and I'm not proud of it. But it's over and it will never happen again."

That's the only thing I can ever remember saying on the air that I wish my mind could have slowed down my tongue.

"Hello everybody...I'm George Kell," I started all the telecasts, "along with my cohort, Al Kaline."

I changed my introduction two or three times over the years. I always wanted something simple and straight to the point. By introducing us right off the reel, I figured we could move right into the action and give the fans what they wanted.

Over the years I've been blessed with the best crew of partners that any broadcaster could ask for. It wouldn't be fair to rate one over another. All of them were professionals. Each one brought his own particular strength that helped me to become a better play-by-play man and make each telecast a little bit better. To all of them, I owe a great debt of gratitude.

Two, in particular, mean a lot to me. Not only as outstanding professionals, but also as lifetime friends.

I learned more about broadcasting from Larry Osterman than anyone I ever worked with. Larry and I were partners from 1967 through 1977. We had a lot of fun and he taught me something new about the profession every time we worked a game.

I respect Larry so much because he came up the hard way. He was not a former professional athlete. He learned his profession the old-fashioned way.

He used to produce sports shows out of the studio. He had to write the scripts, do all of the engineering and then appear on camera looking as fresh as if he had just walked off the golf course after shooting two-under par.

Larry was so smooth with the way he would toss a segment over to me. It never mattered what the situation was. He handled everything I threw his way like an all-star shortstop. I never saw that man walk into the booth unprepared. He did his homework before a game and then he did more work after the game.

Larry may not have known all of the little ins-and-outs of the game like a former player might. But he was such a professional and always so prepared that he put most former players to shame.

He even had a little experience with all of the wiring that goes into a telecast. If we went off the air for a few seconds, he got busy in the booth hooking us up right quickly so we didn't miss too much of the action.

Larry was a great teacher of broadcast techniques. He did it in subtle ways. He never made it feel like he was preaching to me.

He had a whole lot more actual broadcast experience than I had. But he never held that over my head. He just wanted to be part of the team. We were in it together and each one of us knew our roles.

Al Kaline is one of my best friends in the whole world. It was a pleasure working with him because he knows and cares so much about the game.

When Al first started broadcasting, I think he felt a little insecure. That's natural. He was such a great player and always performed to such a high level, I think he wondered if he could meet such high expectations in a new profession.

Al was afraid he might hurt someone's feeling in the clubhouse. He knew all of the players' wives watched the games. He was concerned they'd get upset and tell their husbands about something he might say. He wanted to be friends with everybody.

"You can't do it that way," I told him. "You can still be friends with the players. But you have to report the games the way they are played. You don't have to single someone out and persecute him. You don't have to say so-and-so isn't doing his job. If so-and-so makes an error, though, you have an obligation to tell the truth. You're not up there to cover up. You're not a shill. You're a professional broadcaster."

Al Kaline is not the type of person who would deliberately embarrass someone under any circumstances. He's too much the gentleman.

Because Al knows the game so well, though, he's able to analyze when a player makes a mistake. Al also is quick to point out some little good thing that a player does to help a team that a fan might not even notice.

When I first knew Kaline as a player, there had been some talk about him possibly becoming a manager when his career was finished. To be honest, I never thought of him as managerial type. Even after my first year in the booth with him, I wasn't convinced he would have made a good manager. My opinion changed, though. After spending more time with Al, I'm convinced he could have managed the Tigers and would have done a terrific job.

Al Kaline knows baseball like no one else knows the game. And I witnessed an incident in the clubhouse that proved to me he had the guts to manage a team.

Before a game, Kaline and I were in the Tiger clubhouse when Kirk Gibson started to needle Al about something he had said on the air about Gibson the previous night.

Al can take good-natured ribbing as well as anyone. When it reached a certain point, though, Al put a stop to it in a hurry.

"You do your job as well as I do mine and we won't have any problems," Kaline told him. "All I do is report what happens on the field. You made a mistake and I reported it. There's no hard feelings." Gibson got quiet quickly because he knew Al was right.

Al Kaline would have made a good manager. I'm glad he chose the broadcast booth, though, because it was an honor to work with him for all those years.

Once in a while, Al would go quiet on me. When he saw too many bad plays happening in front of him, it seemed like he got bored with the game.

I learned how to draw him back in. I'd say something like, "That was quite a play in right field. I never would have thought about throwing the ball back here."

Then Al would take over. He'd explain the play from A to Z. He's that smart about baseball.

It truly was a pleasure and an honor to work with Al Kaline. I respect the manner in which he worked his way into becoming a first class broadcaster. He was always prepared and no one knows more about the inside of the game.

Toward the end of my broadcast career, Jim Price was added to the "Kell and Kaline" team. I had never worked with three men in the booth before, but I must say that Jim was a pleasant addition. I respect how hard he worked at his job. I also very much respect the loyalty he he has always shown to the Tigers.

Just as it takes teamwork for any club to excel on the field, a good broadcast requires the same kind of effort from the entire crew. Not just from the announcers, but also from the directors and producers and all of the people behind the scenes.

Over the years, I feel as though I was blessed with some of the best in the business. I hope they feel like I gave them a little something because I feel like I took more than I was able to give in return.

To all, I will remain forever grateful. The one thing they always got from me . . . I was always George Kell.

CHAPTER EIGHTEEN

THE YEAR OF THE TIGER

A ny broadcaster will tell you it's more fun to work with a winning team than one that can't find its way out of the second division.

That's not a case of being a homer. It's a simple case of common sense.

In my last year of broadcasting, we lost on a regular basis. We didn't just get beat, we kept getting walloped, 10-1 or 13-2, or some ridiculous score that looked more like a softball game than baseball. Right from the get-go, we didn't have a chance.

Whether we won, lost or simply got hammered, I still tried to report the games on a consistent level. I just reported the game as it went along. I didn't try to hype it when we won and I didn't try to downplay it when we lost. Win or lose, I tried to make it the same.

I didn't want the fans to say that Kell is making alibis or that he's trying to paint a pretty face onto something that was really ugly. If people had said that, it would have bothered me a lot. I always wanted for them to say at the end of a telecast that Kell reported the game exactly as how it was played. I'm proud to say that my mail reflected that.

That last year got particularly boring. I think that's one of the major differences between working with a good team and a bad one.

When you're working with a winning team, before the first pitch is even thrown, you feel there's going to be a good game regardless which team wins. Blowouts aren't a whole lot of fun, whether it's the Tigers getting blown away or they are bombing the Yankees or Red Sox or anybody else.

A good team makes you feel that there's going to be an honest to goodness game for nine innings. Even if that team falls a couple of runs behind early in the game, there's a feeling that things will get tight by the eighth or ninth innings.

Good teams have a way of creating suspense. In turn, suspense leads to exciting broadcasts for both the fans and the broadcasters.

For most of my career in Detroit, we were blessed with teams that at least kept the whole season interesting. There were some bad clubs, but usually the Tigers fielded a fairly competitive team.

The Tigers always had some individual stars who were exciting to watch. And even toward the end of Sparky Anderson's career when the team was on the down side, Sparky had a way of somehow keeping a team in the race all the way till September when it had no business being there after the Fourth of July.

For a player or a broadcaster, there are no words to describe the excitement of participating in a World Series.

That World Championship of 1968 actually started to take form in 1967. It was such a bizarre season. Not only in the American League pennant race, but throughout the entire nation.

We were telecasting a game in Detroit that Sunday afternoon when the civil riots erupted. I remember looking out over the roof of the stadium during the game and watching this big billow of smoke coming from only 12 or 15 blocks from the ball park.

No one knew for sure exactly what was happening. There was just this eerie foreboding feeling. Something strange was going on, but no one realized how serious it would become. Here we were smack in the middle of a pennant race playing our hearts out, and right up the street the city was burning.

I'm neither a politician nor a moralist. But again I was disheartened by the inability of our nation to do the right thing. As educated as our society had supposedly become, we still couldn't figure how white people and black people could live together.

Again, I thought about Jackie Robinson and all the other black players who were finally allowed to play in the major leagues after years of being snubbed. That had been 20 years prior and still our society had not resolved the bigger picture.

It was a scary time for Detroit and a humiliating period of American history. It's been written so often how the 1967 and 1968 Tigers helped to bring a city together. I don't want to overstate its importance, but I do believe those teams did as much for healing the city as a ball club possibly could do.

At least for a short time.

On the field, the Tigers were locked into the tightest pennant race in American League history. Four teams had a shot to win as the season wound down to its final days.

The Tigers should have won the pennant in 1967. I never publicly criticized or second-guessed a manager. Frankly, though, I thought that Mayo Smith might not have managed it right. In my own mind, I don't think he handled those last few games properly.

The Tigers ended the season with a pair of doubleheaders against the California Angels on the last two days. The Angels deserve a lot of credit. They played as if they were in the World Series. Jim Fregosi played great at shortstop and hit everything thrown at him right on the nose. So did Don Mincher. But we still should have won all four games. We were ahead in each one and finished that weekend with only two wins.

We won the first game on Saturday. We were leading the second, when I believe Mayo left Hank Aguirre on the mound too long.

Aguirre was always a battler. Even when he didn't have his best stuff, Hank gave you everything he had every time he took the ball. Hank had been struggling all day and still had a lead.

Around the seventh inning, Hank fumbled a slow roller back to the mound. He finally picked it up and threw wildly to the plate as the tying run scored.

And Mayo just sat there.

Mr. Fetzer and I happened to be staying at the same hotel. I was eating dinner in the restaurant after the doubleheader when he happened to enter and came to my table.

"George, wasn't that second one the worst ball game you've ever seen?" he asked.

Mr. Fetzer was not one to voice criticism, but I immediately sensed he was thinking the same thing as I had.

"Don't you think we should have had another pitcher in there in the late innings?" he asked.

"Absolutely," I answered.

"Mayo just sat there," he said. "He didn't make a move."

There was nothing more to say. We won the first game on Sunday. We had Denny McLain pitching with a 4-1 lead in the second, but the Angels kept gnawing back to win. The Red Sox won their final game and the Tigers finished one game back.

After that finish, the Tigers were determined to go all the way the next year. They promised themselves right then and there that in 1968, nothing would stop them from playing in October.

We came back with basically the same club. We jumped out of the gate fast . . . we should have won . . . and we did win.

If I have one regret from my playing career, it's the fact that I never had the opportunity to play in a World Series. Every player wants to get that chance at least once in his career. So getting into one as a broadcaster for the Tigers was very special to me. Especially because we played the St. Louis Cardinals and beat them after everyone had pronounced us dead. The Cardinals had been the team I followed all the years I was growing up in Swifton. The St. Louis broadcasts have always been carried in Swifton because it's only about 250 miles away.

The Cardinals had as good a club or even a touch better than the Tigers. They also had World Series experience from 1964 and 1967 with practically the same club.

When we fell behind, three games to one, there were a lot of people who never thought the Series would even head back to St. Louis. Even after we evened it at three, the Cardinals were sending Bob Gibson out for Game Seven.

I broadcasted the games from Detroit and Ernie Harwell did the ones from St. Louis. Charlene and I sat in the stands in the Tiger box for Game Seven. We sat with Alex Callam who was the Tiger treasurer.

Early in the game, I told Callam I was fearful Gibson was going to beat us. Gibson already had pitched in the seventh game of two World Series. When you had just one game to win and everything was on the line, a manager could do no better than to send Bob Gibson to the mound.

"It's a crying shame with (Mickey) Lolich pitching as well as he is that he has to go up against Gibson in this game," I told Callam.

Then in the seventh inning when Jim Northrup hit that line drive over Curt Flood's head to break up the scoreless tie, I was convinced we would win based on the way Lolich was pitching.

After the Tigers took the lead, Flood led off and reached base safely. And that's when Lolich put an exclamation point onto his performance.

Lolich quickly picked Flood off base. He sent a message to the Cardinals that must have chilled all of St. Louis. When he picked Flood off first, Lolich was telling them that he was in command. He told them without saying a word—you might get on base, but that's as far as you're going . . . this game is mine.

I was so nervous throughout that whole World Series. When it was finally over, I felt as proud as if I had batted third in the lineup and won the MVP. That nucleus of players stuck around with the Tigers for several years and became some of the most memorable characters in franchise history.

Al Kaline was the best player on the team. He had been for several years. This was his only chance to play in the World Series and he made the most of it. He batted .375 and sent the Series back to St. Louis with a clutch run-scoring single in Game Five.

Ironically, Kaline almost didn't get the chance to play. He had been hurt a lot during the season. The outfield of Willie Horton, Mickey Stanley and Jim Northrup was very strong. Mayo Smith pulled a rabbit out of his hat when he moved Stanley from center field to shortstop so that he could get Kaline into right.

I didn't know a thing about the switch. No one did. Mayo deserves all the credit for having the guts to make such a move. We wouldn't have been hurt if Ray Oyler had stayed at shortstop. He wouldn't have hit a lick, but he would have gobbled everything up. Hurt or not hurt, though, Kaline had to be in the lineup. He was our best player and actually symbolized the Tigers.

Lou Brock led off the Series for the Cardinals and the first ball he hit was a grounder to Stanley's right. When that ball started to short, I said to myself, "Dear God, please let him come up with it."

And he did. Stanley took a couple of steps into the hole and then fired to first for the out. I think that play helped to settle Stanley down. Maybe it did more for me because I was so nervous I could hardly stay in my seat.

Stanley was the best pure athlete on the team. In fact, he was, by far, one of the most natural athletes I've ever seen. He was as good a center fielder as I've ever seen. He ranks right up there with Joe and Dom DiMaggio and Jimmy Piersall.

For flat out going and getting a ball, Stanley had no peers. He wasn't fast, but he was quick and had great instincts. But he could never discipline himself into becoming a good hitter.

After a game one night, we were flying from one city to another. Mickey had had a bad night at the plate. He was down and looking for help.

"George, you played this game a long time," he said to me. "What do I do wrong at the plate? I just can't get that big hit. With the bases loaded, I just freeze."

In the game that night, he had grounded out with the bases loaded on the first pitch.

"That first pitch was a curveball in the dirt," I told him. "Were you looking for a curveball in the dirt?"

Of course, he wasn't.

"In a situation like that, I just swing," he answered.

Mickey very much wanted to help himself.

"If you go up with the bases loaded, tell yourself you are not going to swing unless you get a fastball in exactly the place you are looking for it," I said. "If it's there, hammer it. If not, let it go.

"The count may get down to 3-2 and now it's you and the pitcher. In that case, you look for a fastball. If you get a curve, you still have time to foul it off. You must have a plan of attack before you go up there."

Mickey could have been a better hitter, but nobody touched him in the field. And he was one of the funniest guys to be around. He was good for the team.

The other regular outfielders were Jim Northrup and Willie Horton.

Northrup had a great year in 1968. I believe Jim was a better player than people gave him credit for. He was a good outfielder, threw extremely well, hit for a decent average and also hit for power.

I think Northrup came along at the wrong time. He could have been a star with a lot of teams. When Kaline was healthy, he was going to play. So was Horton in left and no one could afford to lose Stanley's glove in center. Northrup had to play his career in the shadows of Kaline and he didn't have a chance.

Horton got the chance to play, but I think he was affected by those same shadows. Willie was raised right down the street from the ball park. I think there was a lot of pressure on Willie, and he may not have gotten the credit he may have thought he deserved.

Willie had awesome power. It was the kind that made you stop and watch in wonder when he unloaded on a pitch. I think he was a better outfielder than most people gave him credit for. Mayo took him out a couple of times for defense late in a game in the World Series and that hurt Willie very much.

You could talk about Norm Cash all day and still not tell all the stories. One thing for sure is all of them would be funny ... and most of them true.

At first, I thought Norm should have taken the game a little more seriously and worry about things a little more. Then I got to thinking that if he had done that, he might not have been as good a player as he was. And he was a very valuable player for the Tigers for many years.

When he first came to Detroit, I thought Cash was a very average player. He was much more than that. He came up with so many clutch hits. We couldn't have won in 1968 without him.

The right field seats in Detroit were made for Norman. His swing was custom made for that short upper deck porch. He was the best I've ever seen chasing down pop flies into the right field bullpen. He caught them like a lizard snatches flies with its tongue. He caught them over his shoulder on the dead run and made it look routine.

The second baseman was one of my favorite people. I love Dick McAuliffe. Mac didn't have all the natural talent that a lot of players had, but he was a tough, hard-nosed kid who got every ounce out of his ability.

He could hit. He could run. He wasn't the greatest second baseman, but he played the position as though his life depended on it. That's the way he approached every game. He was a little dog with a big bite. Dick McAuliffe is the kind of guy you win with.

Ray Oyler was so good at shortstop that the Tigers didn't care what he hit. Of course, those Tigers had enough firepower to carry someone like Oyler. I think every winning club has someone like an Oyler. He earned his money; he never had to back up to the paycheck window.

At the plate, Oyler might have done better with his glove. Every player once in a while goes "oh-for-four" or "oh-for-five" a few games in a row. I remember reading one story where Joe Falls wrote that Ray was taking "oh-fors" to a new level. He was "oh-for-August." It didn't matter with Oyler. He was the rock of the infield defense.

Don Wert was a much better player than Oyler because he could hit a little. He had a good glove and was a good enough hitter to play in a lineup that featured guys like Kaline and Cash and Horton and all the rest of them.

On an average team, though, he couldn't hit enough to play regularly. Don was such a wonderful person to be around and he helped that '68 team a lot. But I think he was a little timid at the plate. He didn't dig in deep enough. Pitchers could move him back and not have to worry all that much.

Bill Freehan was the unofficial leader of that club. Kaline was the best player, but Freehan sort of took charge of the leadership.

Bill has always been well spoken. He's articulate and not afraid to take charge. Guys like Horton and maybe even Northrup made more dramatic contributions than Bill. Bill just sort of gave everyone the feeling that everything was under control when he was on the field. That's critical to a winning team.

Freehan caught every day. You couldn't get him out of the lineup if you knocked him over the head with a bat. He was always getting hit by pitches. His left arm swelled up early in the season and stayed that way all year long because he kept getting hit. He was always there, though. I can still see him trotting out to the plate for the start of a game. When he did, the rest of the team knew he was ready and it was time to play ball.

The big individual story of 1968, of course, was Denny McLain. For one year, that's the best season I ever saw a pitcher put together.

To be honest, I was a little disappointed with Denny that year. He won 31 games with a couple of weeks left to play in the season. Then he missed a couple of starts.

It was as though he felt like he had reached his goal, now he was going to skate. I said to myself, "Man, you can win 35 and really leave a mark on the game." Unfortunately, Denny chose to leave his mark in other ways.

Denny wasted a great life and a great career. I feel sorry for him and his family. Denny is a nice guy. He had enough charm to match his fastball. But Denny McLain did not have his priorities in order.

Denny wanted to be a multi-millionaire. He wanted to own his own jet. He wanted to fly to some island for a weekend and then come back on Monday and go to work. He wanted to be very rich and live that fast-lane kind of lifestyle. He was making $100,000 a year when that was a lot of money. And he wound up broke.

I honestly didn't know about all the stuff that was going on around Denny off the field. I didn't find out anything about it until Johnny Sain mentioned something to me. Johnny had been our pitching coach and lived near me up in Walnut Ridge during the off-season.

Sain said he had been contacted by a writer from *Sports Illustrated*. The writer was working on a story that linked Denny to gambling and organized crime.

I told John I didn't know a thing about it. Looking back, though, it didn't surprise me. Nothing did when it came to Denny McLain.

Denny got all the headlines. All Mickey Lolich did was take the ball every time it was his turn to pitch.

Mickey not only was the MVP of the World Series for winning three games, he also was one of the most underrated pitchers in major league baseball almost throughout his career.

Mickey never missed a start. He was the best friend any manager could have. He never gave you a really bad performance. Even in the games he lost, he pitched well. And when he did lose, there never was an alibi. Mickey Lolich had a rubber arm and just kept coming at you till you dropped.

McLain was flamboyant. He got all the headlines and deserved them in 1968. He was a great pitcher with all the confidence in the world. If he had a one-run lead in the seventh inning, the game was over. You could head for the parking lot and beat the crowd.

Lolich was a blue collar sort of guy. He showed up to work every day and never left early. He really was one of the best-kept secrets in either league.

Every player on that 1968 team contributed in some way. Gates Brown was one of those guys who was always called on in the toughest situation. More often than not, he did something good to help the Tigers.

Fans don't realize how tough it is to be a successful pinch hitter. Generally, everything is on the line; there's no second shot. It's one time and out. The Gator was a clutch performer. He had guts and was one of the best teammates anyone had in the clubhouse.

For baseball, and particularly Detroit, 1968 was a critical year. I'm proud of the little part I was privileged to play. In return, I received memories for a lifetime.

CHAPTER NINETEEN

THE SECOND TIME AROUND

N o one figured it would take 16 years for the city to celebrate another World Series championship. When the
1984 season finally ended, it was well worth the wait.

There are similarities between the 1968 and 1984 Tiger teams.
Both were assembled primarily from the Tiger farm system. Both
featured plenty of individual heroics. The success of both was mainly
the result of incredible teamwork. But there also are some striking
differences.

In 1968, almost everyone expected the Tigers to at least make
it into the World Series. After the 1967 heartbreak and with the
nucleus of that team hungry, there was no way to stop the Tigers.

The 1983 Tigers showed signs of maturity. The Tigers were
getting closer to a championship. No one in baseball, though, could
have ever expected them to jump out of the chute the way they
did and then almost stroll all the way into the Playoffs.

This was my second round with a world champion club and
I loved every minute as much as I did the first dance.

Baseball continues to be amazing. Every time we are convinced that a certain record will never be broken, someone jumps
up and pulls off what we thought was impossible. Pete Rose not
only caught Ty Cobb in hits, he left him in his shadow. I never
thought anyone would ever come close to Lou Gehrig's consecu-
tive games played record. Now Cal Ripken, Jr. looks like the eternal
flame.

What the Tigers did at the start of the 1984 season may not
be an official record. But I don't believe we'll ever see another
team win 35 of its first 40 games. At least not in our lifetime.

Right off the reel, the Tigers jumped so far out in front they flew off the radar screen. By Father's Day, everyone in baseball had quietly conceded the East Division to the Tigers. They went 35-5 and made it look easy. It was one of those years when nobody could do wrong.

That season was so much fun for the fans. They got stung by pennant fever early. As early as June, they were looking toward those games in October.

It wasn't that much fun for Sparky, though. No one will ever know how much pressure that man had to feel until the Commissioner handed him the World Championship trophy in the clubhouse after the fifth game.

Can you imagine how he would have felt if the Tigers hadn't won everything after going 35-5? It wouldn't have been right, but a lot of people would have laid the blame squarely on his shoulders. It would have been labeled as one of the biggest "tight collar" jobs in baseball history.

No one had to worry, though. Sparky and every player on that team played and felt like a champion all year long.

It was such a phenomenal season. Every time it looked like the Tigers might be slipping into a little losing streak, some new hero would jump up to stop the slide before it got serious.

When I say everybody contributed, I mean everybody at some point chipped in with something to complete the dream. That right there is a tribute to Sparky. The players won the championship. Sparky is the first to give them credit. But he had every person on that team prepared to play every day.

The Tigers had weathered their rebuilding process and proved without a doubt they were the best team in baseball. That 35-5 start was no fluke.

That team was comprised basically of players developed in the Tiger farm system. Under Mr. Fetzer and Jim Campbell, the Tigers believed in building from within; I happen to agree. There's a tremendous sense of accomplishment when you get to see young players work their way up through the system all the way to a world championship.

From that whole batch of home-grown stars, Alan Trammell and Lou Whitaker will always be favorites because it seemed like they played for the Tigers forever.

As a former player, I still can't believe they played together for the same team for their whole 20-year career. I was a player who was traded four times. That may have been more than most players, but it happens more often than a player sticking with one team his whole career.

As a broadcaster, I got as spoiled as the fans. When a ground ball was hit to shortstop or second base, I knew Trammell and Whitaker would be there. When the Tigers absolutely needed a double play to get out of a jam, I expected those two to turn one.

And just like all the fans, I was rarely disappointed. One way or another, they were going to turn it. They were an absolute pure joy to watch. They could turn a double play in their sleep.

There had never been a combination that good that played together on the same team for 20 years before Trammell and Whitaker came along. I don't believe we'll ever see it again.

Whitaker amazed me because he didn't have that burning desire to be great. He was great because he had so much natural ability. He never had designs on becoming a great player. He didn't want the press to bother him; he didn't want write-ups in the paper. He just went out and did his job.

I'm not sure how many people noticed, but he didn't take batting practice and infield all the time in the 1984 World Series. That wasn't important to him. He just went out onto the field and said to himself, "Let's play the game. I'm going to get a base hit the first time up ad I'm going to make a great play in the infield."

Lou threw as well as any second baseman I have ever seen. He could go deep behind the bag and fire it over to first as easy as lobbing a ball to a child.

Lou was a joy to watch. He had more natural talent than Trammell but not as much desire for greatness. That desire is what made Trammell stand out.

Alan worked hard. He had to work hard to become a good ball player. He learned how to play every hitter in the league. He learned his own strengths and recognized his own limitations. He knew how to play within his own abilities. It's so important for a player to understand his talents and not try to do things he's not capable of doing. The beautiful part about Trammell is that he made every play look routine. That's the sign of a good shortstop.

Alan was a better ball player than I ever was and I realized what he was going through out there. He should wind up in the Hall of Fame. Whitaker wanted to be great, but he knew he could do it without really working.

At third base, I really came to appreciate Tom Brookens. He was not blessed with all that much talent. With whatever he had, though, he gave 100 percent every day. Brookens played hard and wanted to play every day. He got some key hits and played defense fairly well. He was a Don Wert type, but a little bit more outgoing. He was good to have around.

I have great admiration for Kirk Gibson. Gibson probably got as much out of his talent as it's humanly possible to do. He believed in himself so much. He was not afraid to fail. A lot of people are afraid to fail and that's exactly what they do. Gibson didn't have that fear. And he wasn't fearful about how to handle success.

If he struck out on three pitches and looked bad on all three, he didn't let that affect him. He'd bounce back with the winning run on third base the next time up and somehow drive him home.

Gibson was the type of player I wanted on my team when the going got tough. He didn't care about anything but winning. That's all he thought about. That's all he knew.

Particularly at the beginning of his career, Gibson turned off a lot of people with his language and demeanor. But when he took that field, he was focused 100 percent on winning. There aren't too many players like Kirk Gibson. He could play on my team any day.

On the inside, Larry Herndon wanted to win as much as anyone. On the outside, he was as different from Gibson as day and night. Larry has always been so quiet and shy. He was not the type of player a manager built his team around, but he was always there with some big hits.

Larry won the first game of the World Series with a home run. After the game, he grabbed his street clothes and jumped into a cab with his uniform on before the media could get to him. Larry did not need the spotlight. He just wanted to play and was a gentleman all the time.

The Tigers got Chet Lemon from the White Sox in a trade for Steve Kemp. Kemp was a good hitter, but not that good of an outfielder. The trade turned out best for the Tigers, because Lemon gave us some pretty good years.

On the last day of the 1981 season, Jim Campbell called me about the possible Kemp for Lemon trade.

"You know Bobby Winkles pretty well, don't you?" Campbell asked.

I told him I knew Bobby extremely well. Bobby comes right from Swifton. I had coached him in basketball when he was just a boy. He's a fine man. His sister still lives right across the street from Carolyn and me. Winkles had managed in the major leagues and was coaching for the White Sox.

"I want you to call Bobby and ask him very confidentially if he thinks Lemon can help us win a pennant because we're real close," Campbell said.

I called Winkles and asked him to be as honest as he could.

"Chet Lemon will play as hard for you as he possibly can," Winkles told me. "He'll drive you up a wall with his mistakes. He'll try to take an extra base when it's impossible to make. In a tie game, he might lead off an inning with a double and get thrown out at third trying to stretch it into a triple. You'll get so mad at him, you'll want to die. But he plays hard. He's a pretty good center fielder and a pretty good hitter. He's not a star, but I'd take him on my team." I told Campbell exactly what Winkles had said. The deal was made, and the Tigers never regretted it.

Lance Parrish was a lot like Bill Freehan. He developed into the leader of the team. Everyone looked up to him. Everyone felt confident with Lance around.

When he first joined the Tigers, he was so shy he rarely even spoke to anyone. But he grew and you could almost see him maturing right before your eyes.

Lance was so big and so strong. He threw exceptionally well and worked his way into becoming a good catcher. He hit a lot of home runs and drove in big runs. All of his teammates sort of waited for Lance to do something, and he usually did in those days.

In 1984, I witnessed the best single season by a relief pitcher I'd ever seen. Willie Hernandez pitched well in other seasons. For that one year, though, he was untouchable.

I kept track of him all year. When Sparky brought him in to close out a game with a one-run lead in the ninth inning, he invariably struck out the final batter.

He never struggled. He just went in there and set them down. And it always seemed like he finished the game with a strikeout. It was the exclamation point on another save.

In the fifth game of the World Series, Aurelio Lopez relieved in the fifth inning. He simply blew away the Padres with his fastball. I had never seen him throw so well. The game was won and I wondered if Sparky was going to let Lopez finish.

In the ninth, though, there was Hernandez.

"I owed it to Hernandez," Sparky said later when I told him I thought he was going to let Lopez continue.

"He's the guy who brought us to the dance. He earned the chance to finish it."

Hernandez won the Cy Young and the Most Valuable Player Awards for 1984. Still, Jack Morris was the anchor of that whole staff. Of all the pitchers I saw in Detroit when I was there, if I had to win one ball game, I wanted Jack Morris pitching for me. That includes Denny McLain. That includes Mickey Lolich. That includes everybody.

When it got down to winning a big game where everything was on the line, Jack Morris was the man. He proved that throughout the years with Detroit, then with Minnesota and finally with Toronto.

The shutout he fired in the seventh game of Minnesota's victory over Atlanta is one of the greatest accomplishments of World Series history. In fact, it's one of the great pitching performances of all-time. Atlanta was the best team in baseball that year. And Jack set them down without allowing a run. He could have kept pitching into the next afternoon and the Braves still wouldn't have scored.

Jack always wanted the ball. He never missed a start and fought a manager when he was being taken out of a game. When Jack started a game, he expected to finish it. He never looked down to the bullpen when it got to be the sixth or seventh inning like you see so many pitchers doing nowadays. Jack was somewhat of a throwback to the old days of starting pitchers. Jack pitched two complete game victories in the 1984 World Series and it didn't surprise me a lick.

Jack didn't act like he wanted to get along with anybody. Maybe that was his make up and what made him such a better performer than the average pitcher. He always impressed me as a person who felt insecure in a crowd. He felt uncomfortable with a group of people. He preferred hanging with one or two people and probably was closer to Trammell and Gibson than anyone else.

When he took that mound, though, he was in a class of his own. He was fearless. He got better as the competition got better.

Jack loved it in Detroit. He did not want to leave. Money became a factor because the Tigers simply did not hand out those eight- to ten-million dollar contracts. That's the reason Jack left.

Whenever Jack Morris took the mound, I knew for a fact that the Tigers would at least be in the game. He would always give them a chance to win.

I did not do play-by-play for the 1984 World Series. By that time, the networks began to use their own announcers. Al Kaline and I did a pre-game show for Station WDIV.

That whole season was a different kind of ride than I had ever experienced before. There were some differences from 1968. But both seasons ended the same way—with a World Series Championship Trophy up over everybody's head.

CHAPTER TWENTY

ALMOST THERE

T he Tigers made two other power runs at the World Series while I was in the booth. The first came with that nucleus from the 1968 champions. The second came with the core from 1984.

Once you get that taste of being in a World Series, you really want to get back in it. I thought we would make it in 1972. I thought the Tigers had more experience than the Oakland Athletics and that would make the difference in the Playoffs. We came close, just one run short.

The Playoffs had a best-of-five game format at that time. Even after we lost those first two games in Oakland, I thought we would take all three in Detroit.

Our pitching was set up perfectly. We had Joe Coleman, Mickey Lolich and Woodie Fryman going for us.

On the plane ride back to Detroit, I told some people that this series was not over. I figured we were going to get down to a fifth game and that Fryman was going to step up and be the hero. I knew there would be 50,000 screaming Tiger fans in the park for that game. Fryman was used to this and I just had a feeling it would happen.

This was the last gasp for a team that had grown up in the Tiger system and the fans had come to love for so many years. The main differences were that Denny McLain had been traded and Billy Martin had been brought in to manage.

McLain had been traded to Washington in what became a steal for the Tigers. The Tigers got a whole left side of the infield with Eddie Brinkman at shortstop and Aurelio Rodriguez at third. They also got a 20-game winner in Joe Coleman.

Martin joined the Tigers for the 1971 season. Jim Campbell knew the nucleus of the Tigers still had a lot of talent. They had been together for a while, though, and were getting old together.

There still was enough firepower left to make at least one more run, and Campbell felt that his team needed someone to light a fire under it. There was no one better to walk into a new franchise and light a four-alarm fire than Billy Martin. When it came to creating excitement, he was a legitimate arsonist.

In his first year in Detroit, Billy led the Tigers into second place with 91 wins. A player strike delayed the start of the 1972 season and forced teams to play an uneven number of games. When it was over, the Tigers nipped the Red Sox by a half-game to win the East Division.

Between those foul lines, Billy Martin was as good a manager as you'd want. He came to Detroit and did exactly what Campbell had hoped for on the field. It was the off-field stuff that undid Billy the same as it had at his other managerial stops.

Lolich started the Playoffs in Oakland against Catfish Hunter. As usual in a big game, Lolich pitched magnificently. He took a 2-1 lead into the last of the 11th inning before the A's squeaked in two runs. The A's scored the winning run when Al Kaline was charged with a throwing error. It was a perfect throw, but it bounced off the runner's back when he was sliding into third base.

Blue Moon Odom shut out the Tigers, 5-0, in the second game before Detroit woke up to take charge.

Coleman was absolutely untouchable in Game Three. He shut out the A's, 3-0, and set a Playoff record with 14 strikeouts.

Lolich didn't get the win in Game Four. As usual, though, he was a master taking the game into the 10th inning when the Tigers scored three runs to even the series at 2-all.

Now the series got right down to where I had predicted. Fryman started, and he pitched very well. The stadium was packed, but the Tigers fell one run short and lost, 2-1.

The winning run scored after the umpire ruled that Norm Cash had pulled his foot off the bag on a throw to first base. That same play is made a dozen times a game. This time, though, the umpire decided to call it. The A's worked the runner around and that led to the end of the season.

Odom pitched the first five innings. Vida Blue came in and threw nothing but bullets. I don't believe the 1927 Yankees could have hit him that day.

In the last of the 9th, the Tigers put a runner on with two out and Tony Taylor up. I remember I said that as hard as Blue was throwing, I didn't think Tony could get around on him. But Tony always handled the bat pretty well. I thought that if he could just put the bat on the ball, he might be able to poke it into that upper deck in right field. Tony did hit it hard to deep right-center, but it fell just short.

Overall, Oakland had a better team. They were in the middle of that awesome run before Charlie Finley dismantled the club.

As a broadcaster, I really enjoyed that whole season and the Playoffs. That was a special group of Tiger players who still mean so much to Detroit. They always made the games interesting, and they were always fun to be around.

The 1987 team also was special because that was one of the most overachieving teams I have ever seen. Most people didn't expect them to win the division. And maybe they shouldn't have. Somehow they overcame overwhelming odds to win the division on the last day of the season and wound up playing Minnesota for the pennant.

Those seven games against Toronto in the last ten days of the regular season are some of the most memorable games in the club's history. All seven games were decided by one run. The Tigers were left for dead after losing the first three to the Blue Jays. Then they rose from the dead to take the last four.

That was pretty symbolic of their whole season. That season was an absolute joy to broadcast. The Tigers never gave up. Like most Tiger fans, I had the feeling that we already went further than most people thought so why not slip right into the World Series. What's the problem?

Well, there was a big problem—the Minnesota Twins.

Minnesota sort of exposed the Tigers in the Playoffs. A lot of people didn't think the Twins were that good, but they had a very solid ball club. They were much better than a lot of people figured. They defeated the Tigers in five games and actually made it look easier than it probably was.

That Tiger team was so much fun to broadcast ... even more fun than some that won the pennant. Nobody expected the Tigers to win and different guys would keep jumping up to do things no one thought was possible.

Darrell Evans is a good example. He showed me that he was a winner; he simply refused to lose. Late in a game when we needed a big hit, he'd jump up and hit one over the fence.

Evans came up as a third baseman, but hadn't played the position in a long time. When he had to play there in the Playoffs, he took the challenge and made some doggone good plays. That showed me something about Darrell Evans. I have great admiration for him.

Certainly I was pulling for the Tigers to win in both 1972 and 1987. But I was not disappointed with the effort from either one of those teams. They were a pleasure to broadcast and an honor to be associated with. They left me with memories I still feel good about.

CHAPTER TWENTY-ONE

NO MORE LIKE JIM

Baseball is a game that is built on numbers. It used to be that batting average, home runs, runs batted in and runs scored were the most important statistics.

Nowadays, they seem to keep a chart on how many times an infielder pounds his glove before a new hitter steps into the batter's box. With all of their computers, they probably can break it down between right and left-handed hitters.

Statistics have always been part of baseball's charm. They serve as the historical thread from one generation of players to the next. I enjoy studying the numbers as much as any baseball fan. But it's the people in the game that really give the sport its soul.

Maybe more than any other sport, baseball historically has produced a cast of characters large enough to fill a season full of Broadway shows. A lot of those characters seem to blend together. They're basically the same person with a different face.

A very select few are as singular as Ted Williams' swing.

I was privileged to have met a variety of such characters. And without a doubt, Jim Campbell was one of those peculiarly beautiful individuals that I don't believe the game will ever see again.

I believe Jim worked for the Detroit Tigers since the first time Abner Doubleday threw a baseball. At least it seemed that way.

Jim never worked for any other employer in his life except the Detroit Tigers. He joined the organization at one of the Tigers' minor league teams as soon as he graduated from Ohio State University in 1949. He worked his way up to Tiger General Manager in 1962 and ran the club till he was forced into retirement in the middle of the 1992 season.

Whether the fans liked him or not, everyone appreciated Jim's consistency with the Tigers. And whether they agreed with his decisions or not, everyone at least respected his honesty.

Jim was a very special person. He and I did not agree on everything, but I don't believe I ever had a better friend in baseball than Jim Campbell.

Jim died on Halloween night, 1995. The last time I talked to him was the night before he died. Few days ever passed when we didn't at least talk for a brief time on the phone. Not a single day goes by that I don't think about him at least once.

With the direction baseball has taken, the game will never see another character like Jim Campbell again. Maybe the game will produce a different type of character that the fans will still embrace many years down the road. But the Jim Campbell character ended when he was laid to rest in 1995. That mold no longer exists.

Jim ran the Tigers as if the club belonged to him. That was a tribute from the amount of trust Mr. Fetzer placed in him. Jim made all the budgets for every department of the entire organization. He signed every player. He made every trade. He negotiated all the broadcast and concession contracts. There wasn't one aspect of the Tigers for which he didn't exercise final approval.

Jim once explained to me his relationship with Mr. Fetzer.

"If it's anything big where we're going to spend a lot of money or where we are going to trade one of out superstars, I'd like to know about it before the media does," Mr. Fetzer told him. "Just keep me informed. I will not interfere with the deal."

Jim called Mr. Fetzer daily to keep him informed about every little thing that happened to the Tigers. Jim was so loyal and such an upfront honest man; that's why he earned such respect from Mr. Fetzer.

But the game has changed too much for there ever to be another like Jim Campbell. The money has gotten too big. Ball players are signing contracts larger than the national debt of some small countries.

The owners of ball clubs no longer will turn that much authority over to one man. I don't care if it's someone with as much money as there is in the Rockefeller family, the owner is going to make the final decision when it comes to signing certain players. First the deal will have to run through a long line of accountants and lawyers, but it will be the owner who puts the stamp on the deal.

Back in 1976, Charles O. Finley tried to dismantle his Oakland team. He had a legitimate dynasty and no longer could afford to pay all his superstars. He decided to sell his best players to the highest bidder. Finley called Campbell to tell him he was selling four or five players who were the envy of every team.

"I've still got Vida Blue here," Finley said. "Do you want him?"

Anyone who knew the difference between a baseball and a beachball wanted Vida Blue. The sales tag, though, was $1 million. That almost seems like pocket change to a lot of players today. Back then, that represented almost one-third of a franchise's total value.

"I'd like to have him," Jim told Finley. "But this is one I have to run by Mr. Fetzer."

Mr. Fetzer asked for Jim's opinion. Jim told him he'd like to have Blue and Mr. Fetzer quickly authorized the offer. Of course, Commissioner Bowie Kuhn negated Finley's "fire sale." Nevertheless, it was one of the few times Jim felt he ever really needed to get Mr. Fetzer's direct approval to close a deal.

I'm not sure how Jim and I got to be such close friends. It seems that he just took a liking to me even when he worked in the Tigers' minor league operations before he became the General Manager.

I believe Jim appreciated my loyalty to the Tigers. He also respected my playing career and must have trusted my judgment of players. There were numerous times during my broadcast career when he would call to ask my opinion on different players and possible trades. I always was careful never to say anything public about our conversations for two reasons. First, I guess I come from the old school and firmly believe that no trade talk should be made public unless a deal is completed. It's not fair to the teams and not fair to the players involved. More often than not, a trade is not made for a variety of reasons. Why worry players about possibly having to move to another city when, more than likely, the deal won't be made? Secondly, I did not want anyone to think that I exercised any unfair influence over Jim Campbell while I was up in the booth broadcasting the games.

The trade that shocked me more than any other was the deal that sent Denny McLain to the old Washington Senators after the 1970 season. I was at my condo in Little Rock when Jim called to tell me about the possibility.

The deal sounded so impossibly good I thought, at first, Jim was just trying to pull my leg.

"Are you sitting down?" he barked into the phone without even saying hello.

"I'm lying on the floor watching television," I answered.

"Good," he said. "Just lie there and don't get up. I've got something I want to run by you."

After Jim told me the first part of the deal, I couldn't have jumped to my feet if my life had depended on it. I think my legs must have gone numb. It was the biggest deal I had ever heard of.

"Bob Short (former owner of the Senators) wants McLain," Jim said. "He wants him bad."

McLain, at that time, was going through all kinds of suspensions and investigations for a variety of off-field activities that belonged more on a police blotter than in the sports pages.

"Who's he going to give you?" I asked Jim.

There was a slight pause before he answered. Either he still thought it was too good to be true or he was setting me up for a heart attack.

"He wants to give us Eddie Brinkman and Aurelio Rodriguez," Jim said.

"That sounds like a pretty fair deal," I answered. "We need a shortstop and a third baseman."

There was another pause.

"He's going to give me Joe Coleman, too," Jim finally added.

Before Jim finished talking, I told him I couldn't believe it. There was no way in the world he could manage to pry Brinkman, Rodriguez and Coleman out of Washington for McLain. If he did, I told him he was going to be arrested.

"This is like stealing," I told him. "Who else do you have to send him—Mickey Lolich?"

A couple of other players were involved, but no one of consequence.

"Short wants McLain bad," Jim said. "He's hurting for attendance and needs a shot in the arm. He thinks McLain will help."

I told Jim to make that deal before Short had a chance to think about what he was doing. Deals like that come once in a lifetime. Jim could not afford to let that one slip away.

That was a whole left side of the infield with Brinkman and Rodriguez. With Coleman, we picked up a 20-game winner right off the reel. Without that trade, I'm convinced that the Tigers would not have won the American League East title in 1972.

Jim used to call me on a variety of possible deals. I told him quickly exactly how I felt about each one. Whether I liked it or not, I didn't make him wait.

"That's all I wanted to know," Jim would say. Sometimes he would make the deal and sometimes he wouldn't. I was proud that he valued my opinion so much.

Whenever we were telecasting and Jim was on the road with the team, he, Al Kaline, Sparky and I would always go to dinner after the games.

Those were special times for Jim. They also were special for me. If there's anything I miss after my retirement from the game, it's those wonderful nights that will never happen again. They were absolutely priceless. They made all the hassles of travel well worth the effort. We talked about nothing but baseball. I always felt privileged to be at that same table with Campbell, Kaline and Sparky.

A broadcaster from another town once told me how much he envied my relationship with the general manager.

"I have to get an appointment to talk to my guy," he said. "All you do is to go out to dinner with him every night."

That's the way Jim was. If he liked you, you were a friend for life. There was no in-between with him. His loyalty to friends and the Detroit Tigers was uncompromising. Even at the office Jim made himself available to anyone who wanted to talk the business of baseball. His door was always open; no one needed an appointment. He kept his hands on everything that went on with the Tigers.

I believe Jim compromised too much of his personal life for baseball. He was in the office or with his ball club every single day of the year. Holidays or regular work days were all the same to him. It could be ten degrees below zero on a Sunday afternoon in January and he would be at his desk in the office at Tiger Stadium working on something for the upcoming season. His devotion to the Tigers actually cost him his marriage. He had no children. His closest friends in the game became his family.

Jim used to call so much during the winter. Sometimes it was a couple of times a day and almost always late at night. My wife and I would be reading in bed. When that phone rang, I knew it was Jim. I used to answer it in the den because I knew I would be on the line for at least an hour.

"What are you doing?" he'd start.

"I'm lying in bed reading a book getting ready to go to sleep ... that's what I'm doing," I'd answer.

"Well, we've got to talk," he'd say.

We'd talk about everything that was happening in baseball. He kept me informed on every little thing.

In a way, I felt sorry for Jim. I believe he was a lonely man. He lived baseball so much there was really nothing else in his life. When he trusted someone, he talked baseball till it was time to go to sleep. Then he started all over again the next morning.

We didn't agree on everything, but that didn't matter to him. As long as baseball was treated with the proper respect he demanded, he would listen to all opinions.

I think one of the problems facing baseball today is the lack of characters such as Jim Campbell. He not only was a character, he lent character to the game.

There'll never be another like him. I miss him dearly every day.

CHAPTER TWENTY-TWO

SPANNING SIX DECADES

J im Campbell was by far the best friend I ever had in baseball. There are a few other people, though, whom I learned to respect as much as the game itself.

I had admired Bo Schembechler for many years. I had only met him on a few social occasions before he and I were named to the Tigers' Board of Directors in 1989. I got to know him a whole lot better after he was named President of the club in 1990.

Although our friendship really covers only a relatively short period of time, Bo easily is one of the men I most admire in life. Bo has left a tremendous impression on me, not only as one of the most successful coaches and organizers in sports, but also as a caring human being. In spite of that gruff exterior, Bo is one of the most sensitive persons anyone could hope to meet.

Bo demonstrated tremendous compassion while Charlene was losing her battle with cancer. He extended himself in ways that I will remember for the rest of my life.

As a professional, there are few who reach the standards that Bo has established. Not for a moment will I listen to anyone who believes Bo knows nothing about baseball simply because he spent most of his life as one of the most successful college football coaches in history. Bo would have been a winner regardless what path he may have chosen in life.

It's easy to explain why he was so successful. He understands the essence of sports and the importance of organization. More importantly, he knows people. He understands how different personalities function. He's a master at motivation. He quickly recognizes a person's talents and knows how to get that person to perform at his highest level.

A true leader is someone who can analyze a situation accurately ... organize his people to attack the problem properly ... and then stand unafraid to deal with the results. It's impossible to intimidate Bo. The man is fearless; he won't blink.

Bo never asked any of his people to do something that he hadn't already done in some shape or form. And anything he ever asked of his people was always of the highest ethical standards.

Bo Schembechler is a man of extremely high moral standards. He isn't afraid to say what's on his mind—he isn't afraid of any situation. That's why he's such an outstanding leader.

I understand now why he was such a good recruiter when he coached at the University of Michigan. He never promised anything to his recruits that he didn't deliver. He never lied to the parents of those young men. A mother and a father would feel comfortable entrusting their boy to him.

I only wish that Bo would have had more time to serve the Tigers. He was president for only about two-and-a-half years. His tenure came during some of the most turbulent times in club history, which eventually led to the team being sold. Had he been able to stay on the job longer, he would have gotten better and better. He was learning and he was learning very quickly.

During that short period, though, Bo did more to improve the Tigers' minor league affiliates and Detroit's spring training facilities than most people could have done in a decade.

He added coaches to each one of the minor league affiliates. He set up workout rooms for all the farm clubs. He built a batting cage facility in Lakeland, Florida. Anybody who needed extra hitting could go into those cages and swing till his hands started to bleed. The workout building he had constructed next to the clubhouse in Lakeland puts a commercial health club to shame.

Bo became very concerned about improving the Tigers' scouting efforts and free agent draft.

"Why do we draft so high and none of our first-round choices play in the big leagues?" he demanded to know at the first board meeting after he was named president. "That's a one-shot opportunity. We can't afford to miss on those. We haven't had a first-round pick play regularly in the majors since Kirk Gibson."

Bo promised to take it upon himself to become personally involved with signing the Tigers' top selection.

"I'm going to personally talk to the kid and his family to find out just how dedicated this young man really is," he said.

Bo has a certain instinct when it comes to evaluating young athletes. He can measure a young man quickly. He can just look at a youngster and determine how hungry that boy is to succeed.

Before the Tigers made Tony Clark their first draft choice, Bo went to the boy's home in California. He wanted to talk to the young man. He also wanted to talk to Tony's mother and his father.

At first, Bo was not convinced that Clark deserved to be Detroit's top pick. Bo was concerned that Clark also wanted to play basketball in college.

"I'm not sure I want to draft anyone who isn't completely dedicated to this baseball club," he said. Bo did appreciate Clark's athletic ability, though, and finally decided he was the right choice.

Tony Clark is going to turn out to be a great ball player one day, but Bo had to be convinced. He was not merely going to take the word of a scout in California.

Bo is intelligent, hard-working and honest. When he tells you something, you can go to the bank with it. I will never forget his compassion for coming down to Swifton for Charlene's funeral. Ironically, almost one year to the day, he lost his wife to cancer.

In addition to all the personal friendships that I treasure from my career, I was fortunate to have played for or against some of the game's most colorful characters. It was during my broadcasting career, though, that I met one of baseball's all-time characters in Sparky Anderson.

There's no one quite like Sparky. Everybody loves him. All you need to do is to mention his name to get a smile.

As soon as he becomes eligible for induction, Sparky will be elected to Baseball's Hall of Fame. All of the statistics and championships and records he's collected over the years guarantee that. As a manager, Sparky has few peers. The only two managers in history to win more games than he were Mr. Connie Mack and John McGraw.

Sparky's personality is different than Bo's. When it comes to handling people, though, they're exactly the same character.

No manager I ever saw got as much out of his players as Sparky. I saw Sparky nurse what should have been a second division team into a pennant contender. And I saw it happen several times.

He was able to do that because he understands people and treats everybody as an individual. He knew when to pat a player on the back and when to kick one in the behind. He was a psychologist in a baseball uniform.

As for running a game, Sparky was always a couple of innings ahead of everyone. If an opposing manager made one little mistake, Sparky jumped on it like a hanging curve. You had to have more horses than he did to beat Sparky's teams.

Sparky mellowed a little over the years, but I never saw anyone take losses harder than that man. When his team got beat, he looked like he had just lost his best friend in the world. More often than not, he blamed himself for those losses. That wasn't fair because there were a lot of years in Detroit when he hardly had any horses. The barn was bare.

More than all the numbers, Sparky belongs in a class of his own merely for being the type of human being he is. He treats everyone as if that person is a brother or sister. Sparky doesn't go around preaching Christianity . . . he lives it.

He had an enormous impact on the entire Detroit community. He left a tremendous legacy through the establishment of CATCH—his charity which serves underprivileged children in Detroit's inner-city. How many managers or players come into a city and feel as if they have to reach out to the needy before they leave that town for good? Not many.

Sparky felt he had the means to reach out to the kids who need help the most. He knew he better get the job done before he left Detroit. He wanted that charity to live on long after he left Detroit. CATCH continues to serve those indigent kids like few other charities in Detroit.

In all my years, I never was around a more pleasant person. He always was up. He always made everyone around him feel good. And he always was in control of the situation.

Al Kaline means so much to me as a professional colleague and a personal friend. In Detroit, Kaline *is* the Detroit Tigers. Kaline was one of the best overall players in franchise history. Except for Ty Cobb, he may have been Detroit's all-time best.

When Kaline played while I was broadcasting, it was like watching a live baseball instructional film. He did everything so smoothly. He made everything look so easy.

And he could do it all—hit for average, hit for power, run, throw and catch the ball. He used to make a great running catch in the outfield and then throw out a runner in the same motion. The next inning he'd come to bat and deliver a clutch base hit. Kaline knew the game and loved to play it.

He was one of the best two-strike hitters I've ever seen. All the great pitchers will vouch for that. Kaline took charge and made the most of his one appearance in the World Series. Clutch performers like Kaline do not let opportunities like that slip away.

Until we started broadcasting together, I never had gotten that close to Al. Since then, we've become almost like brothers. Al carries himself with so much class. He's a Hall of Famer on and off the field.

Brooks Robinson is a lot like Kaline. Brooks played his whole career in one city and captured the hearts of Baltimore just as Kaline did in Detroit. There never was a finer fielding third baseman than Brooks. I don't believe there ever will be. It's not humanly possible.

Brooks broke in with Baltimore just as I was finishing my career. He took over at third base and I moved over to first. Everyone knew he could field. I just wasn't sure he would hit enough to make an impact on the major leagues. Well, the records speak for themselves. He became a Hall of Fame performer in every aspect of the game.

Brooks was superb at all times. It seemed as though he was able to get just a little bit better with the game on the line. Somehow he always was able to reach back and make a great stop and throw a runner out from his knees. Or maybe fight off several pitches before coming through with a clutch base hit. Off the field, you have to walk two country miles and then skip through a row of corn fields to find a nicer person. Brooks is from Little Rock, Arkansas so there's a natural bond between us. I'm proud to say that Brooks is one of my best friends.

I don't believe any player was as privileged as I was to have worked for three owners like Mr. Connie Mack, Mr. Tom Yawkey and Mr. John Fetzer. I played for Mr. Mack and Mr. Yawkey. Mr. Fetzer hired me to handle the Tiger broadcasts after he purchased the team. In my opinion, during my career in baseball, there was no greater man in the game than Mr. Fetzer.

Tom Monaghan was not around the game as long as those three giants, but Tom was extremely generous to me. I could never have dreamed that I would have the opportunity to serve on the Tigers' board of directors as Tom allowed me to do. He was a good owner and a very decent man.

Because the game has changed so much, we will never see the likes of owners such as Mr. Mack, Mr. Yawkey and Mr. Fetzer again. These are legitimate baseball legends. Mr. Mack molded the game, then Mr. Yawkey and Mr. Fetzer lifted it to a higher level.

One measure of greatness is a man who forges his own destiny. The greats don't follow the paths of others.

Mr. Mack was never a follower. He established his own set of standards and never wavered. I admire Mr. Mack because he believed a successful man could also be a man of dignity and principle. He never was afraid to make a decision and stand behind it, and he never felt the need to express himself in a foul or vulgar manner, even in an environment that was permissive to its practice.

Mr. Yawkey was a different character than Mr. Mack. Mr. Yawkey, of course, never put on a uniform and managed a game. But he loved the game so much and all of the players who played for the Red Sox.

Mr. Yawkey did love to be around "his boys." At times before games, he would be on the field shagging flies or simply "hanging around." Except for Ted Williams, when Mr. Yawkey owned the Red Sox there was no bigger man throughout all of New England. The players loved him. The writers loved him. And the fans loved him. He was good for the Red Sox and good for the game because he cared so much about it.

I never played for Mr. Fetzer. I worked 24 years as a broadcaster for him, though, and learned first-hand that modern baseball owes a great debt to his dedication to the game and his creative imagination.

Mr. Fetzer was the creator of network television revenue sharing for all major league teams. He was a radio-television pioneer. Without his vision, many clubs would have been forced out of business long ago. The mega-million dollar television contracts that exist today might never have happened.

Mr. Fetzer was one of the most intelligent men anyone could imagine. He didn't need the Detroit Tigers for financial purposes. He already was a very wealthy man before he even dreamed about buying them.

Baseball—and particularly the Tigers—was his passion.

Because of his wisdom and business success, Mr. Fetzer quietly became one of the "powers behind the throne" among baseball leadership. When Mr. Fetzer spoke, the rest of the owners listened.

What made the man so unique, however, is that he always placed the overall good of the game even ahead of the immediate fortunes of the Tigers. He felt that if something was good for baseball, eventually it would benefit the Tigers.

That's an incredibly unselfish approach to baseball leadership, especially considering the state of the modern game.

Mr. Fetzer was always particularly concerned about keeping baseball within reach of the average working man. He believed baseball was a family sport and never wanted it to lose sight of its foundation.

As much as any owner of the last half century, Mr. Fetzer left his mark on the game and always in a positive manner. I consider being asked to broadcast the Tiger games by Mr. Fetzer himself as one of the highlights of my career.

The last four years of my broadcasting career were spent under the Tiger ownership of Mike and Marian Ilitch. They certainly had no obligation to treat me as anyone special. When I ran into some health problems, though, they demonstrated how much they wanted to keep me as part of the Tiger family. They went out of their way to make sure I was healthy enough to keep the job for as long as I wanted.

Counting my one game with Philadelphia at the end of the 1943 season, I was honored to have spent 54 years in the major leagues as either a player or broadcaster. I was privileged to share in so many historical eras and events. I have witnessed various changes in the game—some for the good and others for the not so good.

After so many years, it's impossible to acknowledge all of the good people who I've met and who have played such a significant role in my life.

Some of them lived in the daily headlines, working to shape the game so many of us love. Others worked behind the scenes far from the headlines and all of the television cameras. Their impact on the game may have been more subtle. Yet the impression they left on my heart remains as large as any big game-ending home run.

Baseball has always been a game of people. For a little boy from Swifton, I met some of the most wonderful people in the whole world.

And I thank them all.

CHAPTER TWENTY-THREE

TIME AND CHANGE

If you stay in the same neighborhood for 54 years, I suppose it's only natural to see some of the streets take on a little different look.

That's why I'm not surprised with some of the changes baseball has endured since I first broke into the big leagues in 1943. On the field and away from the diamond, the neighborhood remains the same, but some of the neighbors are totally different.

If for no other reason, I believe some of the changes are living proof to the strength of the game's stability. Baseball has to be a beautifully strong and simple game to endure some of the tests we put it through.

On the field, the game has evolved like any long-standing American institution. There have been refinements and adaptations to a changing American society.

Two of the most significant on-the-field changes to occur since when I broke into the majors are the common use of the platoon system and the refinement of the relief specialist. Both of these concepts have radically changed the approach to the game. Not only for the manager and the players, but also for the people who put the teams together and the fans who have altered their expectations from various players.

When I first broke into the game, there were two groups of players. There were the regulars and the utility men. The regulars started almost every game. Utility players were relegated to the bench. They were expected to be ready for any late-inning situation or to fill in for a regular for a few days in case of an injury.

In those days, a lot of the regulars never reported minor injuries to the manager. They simply kept playing. They couldn't afford to sit down. If they sat, they risked losing their jobs. When contracts weren't guaranteed and players had to perform to earn next year's salary, you can be sure that nobody wanted to leave that lineup.

Even the batting orders remained pretty much the same. When I first went to Detroit, Steve O'Neill batted me in the second spot. After I hit .320, he moved me to third, which was the prime spot in the order.

Once I got there, I stayed there for the rest of my career. I never even had to look at the lineup card before a game. I knew I was batting third. And everyone else knew where they were batting.

Casey Stengel started the biggest change in baseball I had ever seen. Casey used a platoon system. He rotated different players into the starting lineup, based upon whether the opposing pitcher was right or left-handed.

Managers must have felt that if it was good enough for Casey it had to be good enough for them. Today managers platoon three or four players every day in an effort to stack their lineups.

For instance, Hank Bauer would play right field against left-handed pitchers for Casey. If a right-hander started, he put Gene Woodling in right.

Of course, Casey had the horses to do pretty much whatever he wanted. Some of those players on the Yankee bench could have been starters on almost any other team. Casey didn't have to worry what his players thought about his system. He stuck with it and those Yankee championships speak for themselves.

Clete Boyer was part of several of those championship teams. Clete was one of the best defensive third basemen of his time; however, there were several players on the Yankees who had a better bat than Clete.

In the 1961 World Series against Cincinnati, the Yankees had a rally going in the first inning. In a World Series, a manager wants to put away a team the first chance he gets. Casey smelled an early kill and lifted Boyer to deliver the knockout punch.

Boyer was hitting seventh in the lineup. Before he even had a chance to bat for the first time, Casey lifted him for a pinch hitter. Boyer felt cheated. He exploded. He tore up a bat rack and everything in his way once he got to the clubhouse.

That never bothered Casey. He had the chance to nail down the coffin and he wasn't going to let it slip away. With his system of platooning players, he always felt he had the upper hand regardless whether the Yankees were facing a right or left-handed pitcher.

Casey also was the first manager I remember who had a relief pitcher designated strictly for closing a game. That man didn't even warm up until at least a couple of outs in the eighth inning.

The Yankees always had a group of starters who were at least as good if not better than most staffs in the league. When it got down to a tight situation in the ninth inning, Casey didn't care who was on the mound. He was going to call in Joe Page and let him finish the game. Page would come in firing nothing but bullets. When he stepped on that mound, it was a signal that the game would soon be over.

That was the beginning of the closer role. In today's game, a team can't expect to challenge for a pennant without a top notch closer.

Relief pitching today has taken on another new dimension. Starting pitchers rarely complete a game. In fact, most of them are looking to the bullpen once they get into the seventh inning. Now there are set-up men to take the game to the closer. It's not the most glamorous role on the staff, but almost every good team has at least one.

Expansion has had a greater effect on the game than most fans realize. Simply from the result of sheer numbers, the talent pool has to be diluted when the major leagues have expanded from 16 to 30 teams.

Expansion has made another impact on the game. Until the early 1950s, travel was by train. The longest trip to the west stopped at St. Louis. Even when I played for Baltimore in 1957, we flew on only about one-half of our trips.

With franchises stretching from coast-to-coast, teams could not play a schedule without air travel. It's eliminated the need for doubleheaders, which are only played to make up a rainout.

Some of the biggest changes involving the game have come off the field, even though their impact might be more far reaching than anything that goes on between the white lines.

Expanded media coverage has definitely affected the overall condition of the game. The modern player can't tie his spikes without someone in the media wanting to know whether he laced the right one first instead of the left.

The media has been good for the game. It's made household names out of some of the most obscure players. But the pressure it creates also takes its toll on players who can't handle it.

Whether any of us likes this overabundance of coverage or not, it's definitely here to stay. And it probably will become even more scrutinizing as competition between various TV networks continues to grow.

While changes in the game remain inevitable and often are good, I am fearful of the direction baseball has taken away from the diamond.

Player salaries have reached a point of absurdity. I think they're dealing with Monopoly money. It's almost make-believe.

That last player strike in 1994 when the owners canceled the World Series hurt baseball more than anyone ever expected. We're still trying to put all the pieces back together. When the owners held out for so long, they vowed we'd never see such monster salaries any more. They were right. The salaries aren't the same. They've gotten even bigger!

I am very concerned with what's happening in baseball. And while I blame most of the problems on salaries, I am not directing the fault at the ball players.

No ball player has ever put a gun to an owner's head and demanded a $5 million or $10 million or $12 million contract. It seems if the player is patient and waits long enough, though, he'll get that kind of salary or at least something close to it.

Maybe it's ego that gets in the way of sound judgment. I know one thing for sure; I wouldn't own a major league club today even if someone were to give one to me.

To compete under today's rules, it seems like an owner has to pay those kinds of salaries. A lot of the fun is choked out of the game when dollar figures become more important than the numbers for runs batted in or earned run averages.

I believe the time has come for owners to say enough is enough. I don't care how wealthy an owner is. He can't continually lose $20 to $40 million a year and expect to remain solvent.

I guarantee you big money men are not in business to lose big money every year. That's one of the reasons we see so many owners selling franchises all the time. There are some franchises for sale now that have been on the market for several years. Salaries have to get back in line. Clubs must start operating within reasonable budgets just as any other business does.

I'm not against any player getting all the money he can from an owner. I would do the same thing. But would you pay Albert Belle $10 million a year to play baseball?

Owners keep trying to devise new ways to generate money. New stadiums seem to be the latest device. New parks are beautiful and can offer fans a lot of fun. Unless a team wins, though, their novelty has a way of wearing off quickly. It happened to the Chicago White Sox, and (owner) Jerry Reinsdorf is a pretty sharp businessman.

Common sense has to return to the operation of the game. Sooner or later owners are going to have to take a stance and tell these players there is a limit to what can be paid.

If the owners told the players we're going to give you $2 million a year instead of $7 million or $8 million and then refused to budge, do you think all those players would simply walk away? I don't think so. Sometimes I think the people running the game actually forget just how much $2 million really is.

I'm very concerned about the economic condition of baseball. Without fair and honest, sound judgment, some of the cities that have enjoyed a major league franchise for years could find themselves without a club.

Change is inevitable. I've seen my share in 54 years. Now is the time to witness some more.

Without the proper ones, I'm fearful that the direction we are currently taking will lead to disaster.

CHAPTER TWENTY-FOUR

BUSINESS AFTER BASEBALL

Early in my career, I started to prepare for when my playing days were over.

When a young major leaguer is doing fairly well, it's easy to fool himself into believing that he is simply going to play ball for the rest of his life. The games will always be there. Retirement is for other players. That last game will never come.

With the way salaries have escalated in sports today, a wise player actually doesn't have to work once he retires. Shame on him if he hasn't taken care of himself and his family for the rest of their lives.

It wasn't always like that, though. Most players, in fact, worked during the off-seasons. Even some of the game's bigger stars had to work to support their families.

I was fortunate. I knew I was going to make Swifton my permanent home, so I took the advice of my daddy and began to buy farm land all the way back in 1949.

"It's obvious you're going to make your home in Swifton," I remember him telling me. "You'd be wise to invest in some farm land. This is a farming community. There's not much else for the average person to do. It's a good investment that will always hold its value."

More than mere security for my family, I wanted to show people that I was not just "a dumb ball player." I could provide for my family in a number of ways. I was a hard worker and not afraid to jump on the right opportunity. I was selective, but that's why I got myself involved with a variety of projects as time went on.

I began by investing in farm land. I bought a few acres here and another few acres there. After a while, I had accumulated quite a bit of good land.

It was a tremendous investment because it secured my future, so I knew we could live in Swifton for the rest of our lives. I was the oldest child. My younger brother, Skeeter, lived about 150 miles from me. My parents and Charlene's parents were getting older. I could see the day coming when we'd have to look over them. That became our responsibility. Investing in farm land provided us the opportunity to live here and do whatever was necessary.

Besides, neither one of us ever wanted to live anywhere else. I liked the idea of knowing everybody in town and being a part of the church and the community. I liked the idea of growing old with my parents and watching my kids go to a small town school. It always seemed a little bit safer.

On top of all that, I've always enjoyed farming. I took a tremendous sense of pride in working with the earth that actually makes up our community. It's good, rich, fertile soil. It's the very soul of Swifton and I loved every part about it.

I no longer can physically work the farm. I rent my land out to a couple of professional farmers, but I spend a lot of time watching over the crops and keeping up with what's happening on my land. I own about 1,100 acres. I raise rice, soybeans, corn and wheat.

There was a time, though, when I came home after a season and I got out in the field to help with all the work. And I enjoyed every minute of it.

I bought the equipment. I hired the help. I went out into the fields and worked alongside them. I raised a lot of cotton in those days, and the cotton was coming up around the time of year I was getting home. It was a beautiful time of year and it was a good feeling to sweat in those cotton fields. Those are fond memories I never will forget.

I've driven a cotton picker. I've driven a combine. I truly liked it. I know what's going on with my farms. When you invest your hard-earned money into it, you keep an eye on it just as you would any other business.

My farms were running fairly well and I was broadcasting full-time for the Tigers in 1962, when I was approached with another venture that had a major effect on my business career.

I invested in an automobile dealership that later became the Kell Motor Company in Newport, Arkansas. My baseball and broadcasting career helped me to secure the franchise. Once I became involved, though, I worked hard to learn the business and make it a profitable investment. I refused to merely put my name on the business and then sit there with my feet on the desk.

Two older local men had been partners in the dealership, which sells Cadillac, Pontiac, Oldsmobile and GMC Truck products. One died and the other—"Biggie" Biggadike—was looking for a new partner.

General Motors did not want to give the dealership to Biggie because he was nearing 80 and the corporation was concerned about what would happen when he passed. GM urged him to find a suitable younger partner.

The regional office for Swifton is located in Memphis. Nearly everyone in the Memphis office, at that time, had been sent there from Detroit and most of them retained their allegiance to the Tigers. Someone asked Biggie if George Kell lived near Newport.

"George lives 18 miles away," Biggie told them. "I know him real well."

The GM people told Biggie that if he could convince me to become a partner, they would be satisfied with the transition.

At first, I was reluctant to get into a new field I knew nothing about. Biggie was persistent, though. He was honest and genuinely concerned with the long-range good of the dealership.

Finally he convinced me I could continue with my broadcasts and oversee my farming interests if we wisely turned the dealership management over to a smart and honest young general manager.

I liked the idea of learning a new business. With my Detroit background, I thought owning an automobile franchise was a prudent investment. We hired a sharp young manager who we could trust with our lives. He ran the business extremely well.

Biggie and I were partners for about five years before I purchased his interest to become sole owner. He had come to me in confidence and told me he was dying of cancer. He felt it would make matters simpler for me and his family if he sold his interest before he died.

"I've got too many children and grandchildren," Biggie said. "I don't want your business cluttered up in an estate. It will be cleaner for you to simply buy me out."

I told Biggie to name a price. He did and the deal was completed quickly.

The business continued to do well. I had outstanding people working for me. I also spent a good amount of time working the dealership myself when I wasn't broadcasting.

Several years ago, George, Jr. returned to Newport to run the dealership for me. Charlene told him that I wouldn't let anyone run anything—I'd always have my hands in it. But she knew I was looking for help and wanted him back in Swifton anyway.

George, Jr. did come back. He dug right into the business and started to make it even more profitable than when I was in charge. He loved the business and all the employees enjoyed working for him.

In 1994, I felt it was the right time to get out of the business completely. I suggested to George, Jr. that he find a partner and I would sell the dealership to them at a price they couldn't afford to pass.

He took on a partner named Dean Sides who is a financial wizard. George, Jr. handles all sales matters and Dean takes care of all the books. It's a perfect situation. That dealership now is more profitable than it's ever been. They move those automobiles off the lot quickly. When I visit the office in the afternoons, those telephones ring off the hook.

The sales agreement I have with them has a 15-year lifespan. They've already offered to pay it off. I told them to go slowly and enjoy the good times. Besides, I enjoy getting that check at the beginning of each month.

I'm very proud of both of them. I'm particularly happy that my son feels so good about being back home. I think when he left to take a job a couple of hundred miles from Swifton, he felt it was the right thing to move away from home. Now he feels as I do. He's home. He's successful in business and I'm so happy to be able to see him every day.

Owning that dealership also helped to open another door that provided me with one of the most unexpected and personally rewarding experiences of my life.

I never have been a politician. But I became politically active behind the scenes with a then-obscure aspiring politician who eventually became one of the most powerful United States Senators in Washington. Through that involvement, I was able to serve the whole state of Arkansas by serving a ten-year appointment on the State Highway Commission.

In 1970, Dale Bumpers was an unheard of small-town lawyer from Charleston, Arkansas, which is clear across the state from me, about 300 miles from my home.

Bumpers was a David in a political battle of Goliaths. First, he had to challenge Orval Faubus for the Democratic nomination. After winning that, he faced the gigantic task of running against Republican Winthrop Rockefeller who already had served two terms and was a very popular governor.

I'm a diehard Democrat, but I have to admit that Governor Rockefeller had done a good job. I didn't think anyone had a chance to beat him.

Bumpers scheduled a stop in Newport to line up support. His campaign people arranged for about a dozen local businessmen to meet with him. He wanted to introduce himself to us and share some of his ideas for the upcoming election.

I had never met Bumpers before. He seemed very bright and ambitious. More important than anything, I was struck by his honesty. He didn't appear to be the stereotypical politician. He seemed to be extremely sincere about the state of Arkansas. I could tell right off the reel that he cared.

"I need your help," he told me. "You know everyone around here and the whole state respects you. Will you help me get elected Governor of Arkansas?"

I was flattered, of course, but I wasn't sure what I could do.

"Mr. Bumpers, I want you to know that I'm involved with the Tiger broadcasts and I have my other businesses to tend to. But I'll do what I can."

As the summer progressed, I became deeper and deeper involved with the campaign. Bumpers worked extremely hard and beat Faubus in the primary for the Democratic nomination. From there he had to tackle Governor Rockefeller and I'm not sure how many people honestly gave him a chance.

I became part of the campaign that traveled throughout the entire state. Headquarters were established in Little Rock. I found myself spending so much time there I asked Charlene if she was willing to spend a few months in Little Rock. She agreed and we purchased a condo. Carolyn and I still spend a good amount of time in it even today.

Bumpers and all of his people worked so hard that they pulled the upset. He was elected governor and my little venture into politics led to a new ten-year assignment.

I was not looking for anything more to do. My hands were full with the broadcasts and my farm and the motor company. Nevertheless, Bumpers called to set up a meeting with me.

"The Highway Commission is one of the most prestigious appointments in the state," he told me. "I want to appoint you to it." I was flabbergasted. I didn't even have an idea that I would be considered for any type of appointment.

"Dale, I was proud to serve on your election committee," I told him. "But you don't owe me a thing. I'm happy that you won and all the hard work was worth it. Besides, I don't know a thing about the Highway Commission."

Some people already had talked to me about a possible appointment to the commission. If offered, they urged me to accept because it would mean a lot to the entire northeast section of the state.

I had told them the same thing I told Bumpers. I honestly was not interested. I had no idea that appointment to the Highway Commission is one of the plum appointments any governor of Arkansas can make. It seemed like everybody wanted to be named to the position—with the exception of me.

"George, there's already about a hundred people who have applied for the position," Bumpers said.

"But I want to appoint you. I can do it without any criticism from anybody. Everybody knows and respects you. They all know you are honest and an experienced businessman. They trust you. I trust you. I want you to take it."

Bumpers said he called about 40 state legislators together to tell them he was going to name George Kell to the Highway Commission. He said he received not one dissenting comment. So I agreed to accept even though I didn't even know where the Highway Commission building was.

That was one of the best decisions I ever made. Serving on the Highway Commission was truly one of the greatest experiences of my life. I learned so much and got the sense that I was truly helping the state of Arkansas. I enjoyed it tremendously.

It's a ten-year irrevocable appointment that continues even if there is a change in governors. That did happen during my tenure when Bill Clinton won the election. That's when I first met the future President of the United States.

There are five commissioners and each one is assigned 15 of the state's 75 counties. Serving under each commissioner is a team of district engineers who have workers reporting to them. The district engineers would recommend to me which roads and bridges were in need of repair or have to be built in the first place.

Serving on the commission is not a position to be taken lightly. The media scrutinizes each move the commission makes. It should. The media is a good watchdog. It checks to make sure that no inordinate amount of money for new roads is being spent in a commissioner's hometown or home county. There's a lot of state money and a tremendous amount of public trust invested in each commissioner.

I'm very proud that not one single negative word was ever written about me during my tenure. I treated that appointment very seriously. I felt as though I not only was representing the Kell name, but also all the good hard working people of the state of Arkansas.

Mr. Fetzer certainly appreciated the importance of my appointment. In fact, when I told him about it before a game in Detroit, he became initially concerned that it may lead to conflicts with my broadcasting responsibilities.

"It's a major appointment," he told me. "Are you sure you can handle it with your busy schedule?" I assured him I was well aware of the situation and had explained it to Dale Bumpers and all concerned parties in Arkansas.

At that time, Mr. Fetzer used to visit Hot Springs, Arkansas quite frequently for vacations. I think he was proud when he would read my name in the local papers in conjunction with my role on the Highway Commission. It showed him that I had a certain amount of respect in Arkansas that maybe he wasn't even aware of.

After serving eight years on the commission, a member is elected chairman. Through an unusual set of circumstances, I served as chairman for the last four years of my commission.

The chairman is expected to make a speech any time a new road or bridge is dedicated. I was always busy traveling around the country on my broadcast assignments, but I'm proud to say that I only missed one meeting during my entire ten years of service.

When my commission expired, the entire work force of about 400 people held a party for me at the highway building. I told them that other than my baseball career, this had been the most exciting experience of my life. I knew nothing about it when I started. I worked hard, though, and was very proud of my service to Arkansas.

If I had never played baseball or never had the opportunity to broadcast, I would have felt that I had made a contribution to something good in my life from my ten years on the Highway Commission.

One of the best results from my political venture is the friendship that developed between Dale Bumpers and me.

After serving two terms as governor, Dale ran against J. William Fulbright for a seat in the United States Senate and beat him. Just as he had served Arkansas so well, Dale went on to become one of our country's most influential senators.

Dale and I have remained close friends. In fact, we're just like brothers. He's a good honest man who demonstrated as much concern for the country as he did for his home state of Arkansas.

That was my lone fling into politics. I have no other political ambitions. It was particularly rewarding to serve my home state. I was re-paid most generously simply from earning the friendship of Dale Bumpers.

My business experience eventually extended beyond my involvement with my farms and my motor company. I served as a director for a bank in Newport for 28 years. I later served for 11 years as a director on a major bank in Little Rock. I also have served as a spokesman for a bank in Lansing, Michigan, for a number of years.

I got involved with everything. It seemed as though at one point, I simply could not say "no" to anyone. Now I serve only on the board of directors of the Farmers Electric Co-op.

The one board I served on of which I am particularly proud was the Board of Directors for the Detroit Tigers. I served as a director for the club from 1989 until Tom Monaghan sold the team in 1992.

That was quite an honor for me. I had played for the Tigers. I had won a batting title in the Tiger uniform. I took tremendous pride in broadcasting their games for all those years. I felt like I was a Detroit Tiger right down to my bones. Yet I never could have imagined I would ever be named to the club's Board of Directors. It was totally unexpected.

Toward the end of 1988, Jim Campbell called me.

"You know, George, we have a board of directors," he said.

"I didn't know that, Jim," I teased him. "I thought you called all the shots."

At that time, the board consisted of four members—Mr. Fetzer, Tom Monaghan, Jim Campbell and Doug Dawson, a long-time Monaghan executive.

Campbell told Monaghan that he felt there should be more voice added to the board.

"Right now, I'm the only person they're listening to," Campbell told me. "I'd feel better if we had a couple more people who know about baseball and aren't afraid to give their opinions."

Monaghan asked Campbell if he had anyone in mind.

"What about George Kell?" Campbell asked Monaghan. "He'll speak up right quick."

Monaghan liked the suggestion. And then he asked Campbell what he thought about Bo Schembechler.

"Excellent," Campbell said. "The man knows sports. The man knows people. He surely knows how to run an organization. And there's no question, he's not afraid to say what's on his mind."

At the annual winter party for the media in January, the Tigers announced that Bo and I had been named to the board. It was one of the highest honors I had ever received in my life.

At certain points during each year, I attended Tiger board meetings. At those meetings, each vice-president of the team made a presentation to the board. I studied hard and learned a lot about the operations of a ball club that go far beyond the games on the field. I'm tremendously grateful for having had that experience. I treated that appointment very seriously and with great respect.

I believe one of the highest compliments I ever received about my business abilities came from Tom Monaghan. He once told me that I brought a lot of prestige and insight to the board. He said he was particularly impressed by the way I analyzed a situation and then spoke up with the way I felt.

I was particularly proud of the fact that the only other former player to be a member of a ball club's board of directors was Stan Musial with the St. Louis Cardinals. That's pretty good company for a boy from Swifton.

Throughout my entire professional career, I always treated my broadcasting duties in Detroit as my top priority. That was the most important position I had. The Tigers had become part of my life. Without them, maybe none of these other opportunities would have arisen.

It was important to me, though, to prove I was more than a ball player. I was proud of my playing career. But I felt I had more to offer. I'm truly grateful for all of the opportunities that were presented to me.

I always gave them my best effort. I hope no one feels betrayed with the job that I did.

CHAPTER TWENTY-FIVE

SHE WAS A LADY

Isn't it funny in life how we sometimes take things for granted? We don't mean to, it just sort of happens. We fall into a routine and go on, day after day, living as though that's the way it's going to be forever. Why should anything change? We like things just the way they are.

We certainly mean no harm. We are all human beings. Sometimes, though, it's wise to slow down a step and take time to count up our blessings.

We don't come into life with any sort of guarantees. We do receive gifts. Some seem to receive more gifts than others. It doesn't matter as long as we are appreciative.

Regardless what those gifts may be ... regardless how many or few there are ... they are ours by the grace of God. And we should be thankful for them each day of our lives.

I was blessed with so many precious gifts. I wanted to become a big league ball player and I was fortunate to play 15 years in the majors. I so much wanted to be inducted into the Hall of Fame. In 1983, that wish came true. I wanted to become the best baseball broadcaster I could possibly be. For 38 years I lived an absolute dream behind the microphone for the Detroit Tigers.

More than anything, I was gifted by my family. I had the perfect mother and father who supported me each step of my journey. Then I was gifted by the most beautiful family anyone could pray for.

My first wife, Charlene, and I grew up together as children in Swifton. I still remember warmly all those wonderful times we shared as kids. That was followed by 50 years of marriage for which I thank the Lord each single day.

My son and my daughter have always been healthy and are blessed with families of their own. George, Jr. lives in Newport, only 18 miles from me. Terrie lives in Jonesboro, only about 30 miles away. We get to see each other often and continue to grow together.

I pride myself on being a religious person. I try hard not merely to attend church services on Sunday. I take pride in serving the Lord by acting as a Christian each day of the year.

As a human being, though, I must admit I took some things for granted. I had always been so blessed and I always was appreciative. But I had never really encountered adversity face to face until 1991. Then I was struck right between the eyes. I was paralyzed by the realization that cancer was stealing Charlene.

How could it happen? Everything had always been so right. Just like everyone else, I understood the eventuality of death we all must face. I just did not understand why it could not have been me instead of Charlene. I was the one who had always been so blessed. No one had ever received so much more than he had given.

So why shouldn't I have to somehow even up the score?

That's not the way life works sometimes. I was crippled by what happened. I would have traded all the good things I was ever blessed with to be able to change what Charlene had to endure.

Charlene and I met in the fifth grade and took to each other like a bee to a flower. We struck up such a special friendship right off the reel that it seemed like we were married all of our lives.

In those days when Swifton High traveled to another school for a basketball game, everyone rode on the same bus—the basketball team, the cheerleaders and all the students. I was captain of the team in my senior year and had a seat that was sort of unofficially reserved for me. No one ever sat down in that seat next to me. That was reserved for Charlene and everybody knew it.

When we were just 19 years old, we were secretly married on May 24, 1941. On August 20, 1991, Charlene died. Our entire lives had been spent together.

When Charlene died, nothing I had done meant a lick to me. Not my baseball career. Not my broadcasting career. Not even being named to the Hall of Fame.

When a person loses his lifelong love and best friend in the world, none of those things that seem so important really amount to anything. At that time, it's impossible not to reflect about all the good times and all the little bumps in the road that they had shared together.

I couldn't help but think about all the sacrifices Charlene had made for me and our family throughout her life.

Being the wife of a major league ball player is not as glamorous as it appears on the surface. While the husband is off playing games all over the country, the wife has to take care of the house and the kids and all the problems that go with them.

As tough as it was on me being traded four times, I know it had to be even tougher on Charlene. Being traded means a family has to pull up stakes and move to another part of the country where everyone is a stranger.

There are so many things to take care of, like finding a new house or a new doctor or dentist. Sometimes the kids have to enroll in a new school. Charlene handled everything. And she did it all without ever saying a word. Not once did she ever complain.

Even later in my career when I began to feel like I should spend more time at home to help raise the kids, Charlene didn't complain.

"What are you going to do?" she would ask me. "You're a ball player. You're good and that's where you make your living."

She understood that if I had left the game too soon I might have regrets later. It wasn't until much later in my career that she was satisfied I could comfortably handle walking away from the game.

"We have the farm here," I told her. "We can make ten or twelve or fifteen thousand dollars a year." She said that if I was sure that's what I wanted, then the family would be happy.

Regardless of my decision, she supported me. I never had to worry if she was going to stand by my side. She was right there. She never wavered.

We began to build the house that Carolyn and I still live in today back in 1946. It wasn't quite finished, but just before I went to spring training in 1947, we moved our furniture into it. George, Jr. was born in 1945 so he was just one year old when we moved in. Terrie was born in this house.

There was a rickety old house that used to stand on this lot. It had probably been there about 75 years. It looked as though if a strong wind had a notion, it could have taken that old house down to the ground any time it wanted. It might have required only a real strong breeze.

The house was owned by Dr. Justice. His mother lived there alone and she died when she was about 85 years old. The house was only a short pop-up from what we call downtown Swifton. Dr. Justice asked if I wanted to buy it.

"I know the house is nothing," he said. "But you can knock it down and start all over. It's got a big lot and a beautiful location." It didn't take long to sell me. We bought the house and started making plans.

An old carpenter used to live next door to that house. I asked him what he would charge me to tear the house down.

"The lumber," he said quickly. "There's a lot of good timber in that house and I'll put it to good use. You let me have the lumber and I'll take that house right down to the ground."

There was a builder who lived up in Walnut Ridge. I called on him and we started him working on the same house that we live in today. We added an upstairs and put on a couple of other additions over the years. But it's basically the same house. Charlene and I both loved that house. She took care of it and turned it into a home.

Charlene loved people. She was always fun to be around. Basically, though, she was a very private and proper person. She didn't enjoy being around people who were drinking and carrying on, and I sure couldn't blame her for that.

She was one of the most generous persons I have ever met. She was always doing things for other people that no one knew anything about.

Charlene served as the superintendent of the Children's Sunday School for the Swifton United Methodist Church. In her job, she would visit families who didn't attend services. She wanted to talk to the kids and persuade them and their parents to attend church. Sometimes she would come home with a little less money than she had when she went out the door.

"George, I have to tell you I wrote a check for $100 to those people," she'd tell me. "They don't have a thing. They haven't been as blessed as us. Maybe if they had some new shoes or better clothes they'd feel more comfortable coming to church." She was always giving away money and gifts. She didn't tell me all the time, but I knew.

By the time she died, Dale Bumpers already had been serving in the U.S. Senate for some years. He had gotten very close to Charlene and my whole family. It wasn't easy for Dale, but he graciously agreed to deliver the eulogy.

"I'm not exactly sure what to say," he told me.

"Just tell the people she was a lady," I told the Senator. "She was truly a lady."

Everyone in Swifton truly knew that. And that's pretty much what he said.

I think Charlene had suspected something was wrong with her long before any of us knew about it. She didn't whisper a word. Maybe she thought if she didn't say anything, it would just go away. We all know something like cancer doesn't "just go away."

As I look back, a few people at church mentioned something to me.

"Are you just going to sit there and let your wife die?" an old friend from down the street said to me.

"What do you mean, Harold?" I asked.

"George, there's something wrong with Charlene," he said. "It's summertime and she wears her long coat all the time. She doesn't want the people to see how thin she's getting."

Maybe I should have grabbed her and taken her to the doctor. But I knew that Charlene would not go.

In that autumn, my daughter, Terrie, visited us.

"Mama cooked a big meal today, but she didn't eat anything," Terrie told me. I thought maybe she just wasn't hungry. Or maybe she had nibbled while she was preparing it.

For Thanksgiving in 1990, the whole family joined us at our house. Terrie again told me that Charlene didn't eat anything. That's when I began to raise a fuss.

"You're not eating anything," I said. "We're going to see a doctor."

Of course, she refused. Terrie, George, Jr. and I watched her very closely. We fussed with her all the time. Finally at Christmas, I confronted her very seriously.

"George, I can't eat," she told me. "I can't get anything down. Even when I do, I can't keep it down."

There was no way for Charlene to argue with us. I insisted we were taking her for an examination. In the early part of January, 1991, I took her to a doctor in Little Rock. The doctor suspected cancer and scheduled exploratory surgery for the next day.

I will never forget what the doctor told me after the operation.

"I dipped cancer out with a spoon," he said. "But we couldn't get half of it. Her stomach is filled with cancer."

I'm not sure anyone can exactly explain what he feels like when he hears those words. You know what the words mean, but you just don't want to believe what the consequences are. I asked the doctor what we were going to do.

"We're going to give her chemo," he said.

No promises were made. My mother had died of a heart attack in her sleep in 1975. Our family had been so close, it was a very difficult time. But it was something all children realize they must face with their parents.

Charlene's condition was totally different. This was the most serious part of life either one of us ever had to face.

When I went to spring training that year, I asked to meet with Tom Monaghan, Jim Campbell and Bo Schembechler. I told them how serious the situation had become. I told them I might not be able to broadcast all the games that year.

All three were extremely sensitive to the situation. They told me to take time off immediately and return whenever I saw fit. I told them I'd like to broadcast for as long as I can and then simply walk away. I had been thinking about quitting anyway. After the meeting, I walked to the park with Bo. He asked if I was serious about quitting.

"I'm getting to the point where I think this might be my last year," I told him.

He was extremely gracious, but cautioned me not to make any long-range decisions at the moment.

Around the middle of June, I no longer could continue the broadcasts. I called Alan Frank to tell him that Saturday would be my last game. Alan is the general manager of Station WDIV which carried the telecasts at the time. His kindness to me and my family is something I will cherish until the day I die.

Alan asked what time I would arrive in Detroit on Saturday. I told him about noon and he was waiting for me at hotel when I got there.

"You take as much time off as you need and do whatever you have to do," Alan told me. "If you need a year, take it. We'll get someone else to fill in until you feel you're ready to come back. You let me know when that time comes."

Alan realized how bad Charlene was. He asked what time was best for him to call.

"I stay at the hospital all day," I told him. "I get home between nine and ten o'clock."

Alan called regularly and we'd simply talk. He was honest, he was fair and extremely compassionate. I trusted Alan like a brother. He will be a friend for life.

As the spring wore on, Charlene kept getting weaker and weaker. The chemo was eating her alive.

One day in June, the doctor told me could not help her any more. The chemo seemed to be doing as much damage as the cancer and he did not want to administer any more.

"At least give her the chemo today," I pleaded. "I don't want to shock her."

He agreed, but insisted she be hospitalized. In the hospital, I told Charlene the doctor could do no more.

"Well, if I'm going to die, I don't want it to be in the hospital," she said. "I want to go home." We spent the last eight weeks of her life in the bedroom. She became so weak, she was unable to leave her bed.

We had the opportunity to talk about everything. She planned her funeral. She told me what she wanted for the kids. There were times when we laughed. Once when I tried to help her out of bed, I slipped and she fell on top of me.

Charlene started to laugh.

"I can't get off of you," she said.

"Well, I can't get from under you," I answered.

We just laid on the floor laughing. It was just a small moment I'll always remember.

She slipped into a coma for the last two weeks of her life. I stayed with her every moment.

On the evening of August 20, I received a telephone call. Before I left the room, I touched her face. It was so hot, I thought my hand would burn. When I came back just a few moments later, her face was cold as ice.

I pulled her next to me and started breathing into her mouth. The doctor later told me I could not have revived her in a hundred years.

It's difficult to remember all that went through my mind. We had had such a great life together. There were no harsh words. There were never any fights. I just couldn't understand why it couldn't have been me.

The ladies of the church did a marvelous job of organizing everything for the funeral. They just took right over. They arranged for a little reception in the assembly hall next to the church.

The preacher knew how big the crowd would be and how small our church is. He put speakers in the trees around the church. There were as many people outside as there were inside.

I told Jim Campbell to tell our friends from the ball club not to come to the funeral. I suggested that they say their prayers from home. August is such a hot month in Arkansas. We didn't even have the funeral till five in the afternoon when it was a little cooler. And I knew how crowded it would be.

About noon, though, I was sitting in my house when two special visitors arrived. It was Alex Callam, the long-time treasurer of the Tigers and a great friend, and Bo.

Bo told me he just didn't feel right staying at home. After all the years I had served the ball club, he said he had to be in Swifton on this day. When he awoke, he called Tom Monaghan and asked for the use of one of his planes.

"I'm going to Swifton," Bo told Monaghan. "I've got to be there."

That's the kind of guy Bo Schembechler is.

There was such a crowd of people in the house and at the church that it's difficult to recall everything that happened.

I do remember thinking about some of the things Charlene and I talked about during her last months. She was so appreciative for all the blessings we were fortunate to have received.

We had married young and it worked. We were blessed with two fine children, six grandchildren and two great granddaughters. We were able to do pretty much what we wanted to do all of our lives. And we were able to spend our lives together in Swifton for more than 50 years of marriage.

She was very appreciative . . . and so much a lady.

CHAPTER TWENTY-SIX

ANOTHER PRAYER ANSWERED

There was a time after Charlene passed that I stayed at home and prayed to God that I would die, too. I wanted Him to take me. That's a terrible thing to say, but I had gotten it into my head that was the only way I'd ever see Charlene again.

God did answer my prayers in His own way. He gave me Carolyn and I thank Him every day.

For several weeks after the funeral, I just sat in that big chair behind my desk and did nothing. Our preacher at that time used to visit me a few times a week.

After he married Carolyn and me, he told her: "I was really proud to minister your wedding. I was fearful George was just going to sit in that chair till he died."

I'm happy today because of Carolyn. She helped me to put my life back together. When we were just about ready to marry, she told me, "I can't replace Charlene ... I just want to make you happy."

That tells you what kind of lady Carolyn is.

I met Carolyn through my association with the local bank in Newport. I had served on the board as one of its directors for 29 years. Carolyn had worked there for 27 years. There were about 25 ladies employed by the bank. Other than to say "hello," I didn't really know them.

In the summer of 1992 when I visited the bank, I used to have light conversations with Carolyn. Carolyn's children already are grown. In 1993 I finally worked up enough nerve to ask her to join me for dinner.

I took her out to dinners periodically for about a year. I suppose one thing led to another until finally I asked her if she wanted to be tied down to an older man and marry me.

She said it would suit her fine and I felt as if a new life had been breathed into me. We married at the Swifton Methodist Church on May 7, 1994 and it was the best decision I could have made.

Carolyn has demonstrated an amazing mixture of bravery and compassion. She's a tremendously strong person with an equal amount of sensitivity.

It's an awful big leap for a woman to move into the home of another woman who had spent 45 years there. There are a lot of memories that still live in the house. Carolyn has handled it with class and a sensitivity that is simply amazing.

As soon as she moved into the house after our wedding, she told George, Jr. and Terrie to take anything they wanted as remembrances from their mother. That's just the way Carolyn is. She did not want to intrude on the kids' memories of their mother. Instead, she's become so much a part of the family.

I was concerned about the relationship between my children and Carolyn before we married. I don't think I would have felt comfortable with someone that they didn't love.

Terrie was cooking dinner for the Thanksgiving before Carolyn and I married. I asked Terrie if it would be all right if I asked Carolyn to join us. Terrie welcomed the notion. I believe that was the start of what really made me feel good because Terrie and George, Jr. both felt so comfortable around her.

Carolyn and I share so many similar interests. Both of us are avid readers. Every night before we turn out the lights, we each have a book in our hands. Since we've been married, Carolyn has become as rabid a baseball fan as I am. Before we married, Carolyn didn't know baseball from hockey. One game or another, it was all the same to her.

Now she knows baseball better than a lot of fans who have followed the game their entire lives. She knows all the players. She understands those who belong on the team and those who should be sent back to the minors.

We have a satellite dish in the backyard that brings us three or four games every night. She can't wait for all the Tiger telecasts. She's become very attached to the Tigers. She knows each one of those players as if she had followed the game for years.

Before we married, she knew I broadcasted games for the Tigers. What she didn't understand was some of the grind that went into broadcast life behind the scenes. She thought doing the telecasts from different cities around the country was almost like a vacation.

Shortly after we married, Carolyn asked if she could accompany me on a road trip. I was pleased that she was interested and we had a great time everywhere we went. That first year, she probably made about 80 percent of the trips. She still enjoyed the travel, but she cut back the number of trips the following year.

"I thought it was going to be a lark," she said. "I never realized how much you have to do."

When we returned from trips, friends asked her where she'd been and at what restaurants did we eat?

"We ate in our room in the hotel," she told them. "George had to go to the park at around four o'clock. By the time he was finished and returned, it was around midnight before we'd finally have dinner."

Like so many people who have never been exposed to the inside workings of baseball, Carolyn never realized the rigors of the game. For those who actually work inside the sport, there are a lot more demands on time than the mere three hours it takes to play nine innings.

Carolyn remained extremely supportive of my broadcast career. She was equally supportive about the possibility of my retirement.

"It doesn't matter to me whichever decision you make," she told me. "You just make sure that you are satisfied with the one you choose."

After Charlene had died, I honestly didn't think there was anything in life to make me happy again. Carolyn never did try to replace Charlene. In her own way, she simply filled a void for which we both are satisfied.

Now I thank God for answering my prayers in His own way.

CHAPTER TWENTY-SEVEN

AGAIN ... IT WAS TIME

T he toughest part about walking away from the broadcast booth for the last time was leaving the fans of
Detroit.

I had been at the job for 38 years. That's a long time even for
a job that is so much fun. And, believe me, I loved every minute of
this one.

During those 38 years, we had a lot of good ball clubs. Some
of them were not so good.

The one thing that never changed were the fans. They were
the best in the country. Everyone wants a winner, but it doesn't
happen like that every year in baseball.

All that the Detroit fans demanded was effort. They understood baseball. They appreciated the game and all of the little things
that go into making it such a great sport.

More than anything else, I always found the Detroit fans to be
honest, down-to-earth, caring people. It's a working-class city. The
work ethic of the whole state is second to none. People like that
are real people. They treated me just like family from the first day I
ever stepped foot into the city.

Twice I had the opportunity to leave the broadcast booth in
Detroit for one in St. Louis doing the Cardinal games. That would
have meant a lot to me because St. Louis is so close to Swifton. All
my family and friends could have listened to my broadcasts. A lot
of them could have made the trip up north to visit me once in a
while.

But I could not leave Detroit. There was something about
that tie between the fans and the ball club that extended up into
the broadcast booth.

There was no way I could sever those ties and be as happy as I was doing the games in Detroit.

Finally, it got to the point where there was no decision to make. After the 1996 season I realized I no longer could physically handle the job.

One lesson I've learned from sports maybe better than any other is that the only thing harder to be than a good loser is a good winner. I felt like I had been a winner all my life in Detroit. I wanted to make sure that was the way I went out.

Late in the 1992 season, my left knee began to bother me. Eventually it got to feel as if it were on fire. At first I tried to ignore it. I guess I was hoping the pain would just go away. It never did "just go away." In 1993, it bothered me quite a bit.

In 1994 it continued to get worse. I knew I could not go on like this. I had trouble walking up to the broadcast booths in the various parks. Traveling around the country got to be a real burden. What started to bother me even more than the pain was the feeling that I could not do my job properly. Al Kaline was so good to me. Many times he would carry my bag when I had trouble moving around.

By that time, Mike Ilitch had bought the ball club. I finally had to call him to tell him the problem. I knew that unless I got relief soon, it would be too late to quit.

I wanted to talk to him privately and in person. He asked me to come to his office immediately and I was delighted.

"I've got a knee that's just bone rubbing against bone," I told him. "I can't even carry my own bag."

Right off the reel he told me that he wanted me to remain with the club. But first he wanted me to do "what's best for George Kell."

"I've always liked the jingle of 'Kell and Kaline'" he said. "I don't want to end it now."

Before I left his office that day, he told me wanted me to meet my No. 1 fan. He took me into his wife, Marian's, office. Mrs. Ilitch then escorted me into an office she called her "Hall of Fame Room."

A wall in that room was lined with pictures of her personal "Hall of Famers." It included a galaxy of stars that had appeared at the Fox Theater which the Ilitches own. The first picture I recognized was Frank Sinatra.

I quickly scanned all the pictures and noticed I was the only ball player on the wall. There were no others. I was shocked and honored beyond any words I could come up with.

I hugged Mrs. Ilitch and shook Mr. Ilitch's hand before I quickly left the room because I could feel tears coming to my eyes. Before that day, I had hardly known my bosses. Suddenly I knew I had made two more friends for life. "Kell and Kaline" —I kind of liked the sound of that jingle, too.

After the season, I had a complete knee replacement. When I told Mr. Ilitch the surgery was successful, he wrote me a kind letter that made me feel the club wanted me back.

"This is good news for George Kell and good news for the Detroit Baseball Club that you're coming back," the letter read.

I felt like a new man until I hurt my back after the 1996 season. Again I needed surgery. My recovery, this time, was not as swift as the first one. My back had gotten weak and the pain traveled down through both of my legs.

The doctor explained the seriousness of the surgery. He said it would take quite a while for full recovery. It got down to the new year and I knew I could not make another season. It was not fair to the club, nor to Kaline nor to anyone for me to start the year the way I felt.

After 38 years in the booth, it was an awfully tough decision. At a time like that, it's impossible not to look back and remember all the good times. Not just all the games and the winning seasons, but all of the good people I had been blessed to work with. I think the thought of missing them bothered me more than the games coming to an end.

When I called an end to my playing career, it was partly due to the guilt I felt over being away from home so much. During my broadcasting career, I had things pretty much the way I wanted them. I was able to spend most of my time at home. So this decision was quite a bit different.

Carolyn was as supportive as I knew she would be. She felt it was time for me to retire. She felt I was working too hard, traveling too much and not enjoying life the way I should. She would have stuck with me broadcasting for another ten years. Down deep, though, she knew what was the right thing for me to do.

"I know that you aren't able to handle all the travel," she said. "If you decide to try, though, I'll help you any way I can."

My kids were a little stronger with their opinions. They wanted me to quit. They wanted me to spend even more time with the grandchildren. Terrie also was so fearful that the next plane crash she heard about would be one that I was on.

"Daddy, when are you going to quit?" George, Jr. kept asking. "When you're 90, or when they bury you?"

When I visited Detroit in January, I told John McHale, Jr. (Tiger President) I no longer could continue.

"John, I'm so sorry," I told him. "I apologize I couldn't tell you sooner, but I thought I would be able to go on. There comes a time for everyone, though, and I guess it's just my time."

McHale understood. He thanked me for giving the club two more years than they had expected after my knee operation.

When I left, I felt like I was leaving home instead of going back to it. I felt like I was walking away from so many good friends. I always felt good about being in Detroit. Even though I didn't live there, I felt as if I was part of the community. That's the way the people always made me feel.

It wasn't until I left, though, that I truly understood how the people felt about me. I was overwhelmed by the letters I received.

I always felt relaxed when I was doing a game. I never felt pressure and I hope I came across to the viewers like that. If I had realized how many people I was touching every night I sat behind that mike, I probably would have gotten so scared that my tongue would have gotten tangled up with my necktie.

I would have loved to have kept on doing the broadcasts for a number of more years. I was confident there was no problem with my ability to call a game. I just had trouble with getting to them.

There simply comes a point when it's time to call it the end of a game. It was my time. And that 38-year run was more than anything I could have imagined.

CHAPTER TWENTY-EIGHT

A TIME TO SHARE

There's a certain magic to the name "Cooperstown" like no other city in any American sport.

Not everyone knows exactly where Cooperstown is located. Almost everyone realizes, though, what that little town means to baseball and the very spirit of our country.

Cooperstown is home to Baseball's Hall of Fame. Even those who don't religiously follow the game understand what a fan means when he mentions he's going to Cooperstown.

Although it had been my goal "to make it to Cooperstown" ever since I was a youngster, I had never even been to that little town in upstate New York until I was inducted in 1983. When I finally made it there, it was the most overwhelming experience of my entire life.

As far as professional accomplishments are concerned, I wanted to be elected to the Hall of Fame more than anything I ever wanted in life. For any professional baseball player, there is no greater honor. For me, in particular, it was a dream come true. Not just for me and my own family, but also for my dad.

This was the dream that he shared with his three boys. Two of us had made it to the big leagues. One had died in the war.

I was able to fulfill my father's dream before he died. For me, that was as great a feeling as actually seeing my plaque up on the Hall of Fame wall itself.

The emotions a player experiences during his induction ceremonies are impossible to put into words. The nearest I can come is a sincere sense of awe.

When I stood up on that stage that Sunday afternoon with all those people in front of me and all those great players sitting behind me, I was flat-out awe-stricken.

Those were legitimate baseball legends up on that stage with me. There was Ted Williams and Joe DiMaggio and Stan Musial and Joe Cronin and Al Kaline and so many others.

Babe Ruth and Ty Cobb and Walter Johnson and all the rest who had passed obviously weren't there. You can be sure, though, that their spirits were present. No one can tell me any differently because I felt them. Their presence was inescapable.

I was inducted along with Walter Alston, Juan Marichal and my long-time good friend Brooks Robinson. Going in with that group alone still sends chills through my body.

Nobody makes it into the Hall of Fame strictly on their ability alone. It's impossible to go that far without the help and support of so many different people.

There are all the managers and coaches that you ever played for, all the way back to American Legion ball. There are all the teammates who gave you a lift when you needed one and helped you to get the most out of your God-given talent. There are so many fans who refused to give up on you even when the going got a little tough.

More than anything else is your family. The family is there for the home runs and the strikeouts ... the wins and the losses ... the glories and the defeats.

That's what made that ceremony so special for me. My wife was there. My children were there. My grandchildren were there. I was able to share that moment with the ones I love most. They were the ones who sacrificed so much so that I could stand in glory for the rest of baseball history. That honor belongs every bit as much to all of those people as it does to me.

In fact, more than to anyone, it belongs to my father. He's the one who shared my dream since when I was just a boy. He refused to give up no matter how hard times would get.

My father was not physically able to attend the ceremonies in Cooperstown. I certainly felt his spirit, though. He watched everything on television from his wheelchair in a nursing home in Newport, Arkansas.

That induction weekend in Cooperstown was the greatest thing that ever happened to the Kell family. Everyone felt that same sense of awe that grabbed me as soon as I arrived in the little town.

I was voted into the Hall of Fame by the Veterans Committee in March of 1983. I'm particularly proud of that because that's a committee of my peers. Those are the fellows who were there when I was playing. They're the same men who won my respect and admiration many years ago.

I knew the committee was meeting on the day I was in Detroit filming a commercial for a Lansing, Michigan, bank that I represent. Earlier that week, I had read a story in the newspaper that I was considered to be a front runner for selection.

When the committee called my home in Swifton to give us the news, Charlene told them I was up in Detroit. We were filming the spot in a private suburban home so no one knew how to reach me immediately.

Early that morning, I had called George, Jr. at the Motor Company from the home where we were filming. I had left the number for the house and thank goodness Charlene called him to find out if he might know where I was.

One of the crew members answered the telephone. When he said the call was for me, I knew right away it was either an emergency or that I had been elected to the Hall of Fame.

"You're a Hall of Famer," Charlene told me as soon as I answered.

I suppose at that moment we both shed a little tear. Then she told me they wanted me to be in St. Petersburg, Florida, the next day. The Hall of Fame wanted to introduce Walter Alston and me at the annual Governor's Dinner.

When I informed the filming crew of the news, they seemed to get even more excited than I had. They shut down the shoot. They said we'd complete it a couple of weeks later. It was time to celebrate. One of the members hurriedly bought a bottle of champagne for a toast.

I raced to the airport to catch an earlier flight home. Before I went to Swifton, I wanted to stop in Newport at the nursing home to share the news with my father.

Ever since I was a kid, he had always been there for me. It was my turn now to be with him at the biggest moment of my professional career. He was the first person I wanted to talk to.

My father had developed Parkinson's disease. His mind was sharp and he could speak as well as I could, but he could not walk. He lived alone for about six years after my mother died in 1975. Finally, he could not handle it anymore and we were fortunate to find this home.

It's located just a few blocks from the Motor Company. I stopped in to visit him every day I was in town. The nurses loved him and treated him very well.

My father never burdened anyone in the family. When he moved into the nursing home he asked only one favor. He wanted me to take him to church every Sunday morning that I was in town. That was so important to him. And also to me. I was proud to make that promise.

When I arrived at the nursing home that afternoon, he was dressed in his "Sunday go to church" suit. He looked like a million dollars. He knew that I would come.

By the time I arrived, he already had heard the news. It was a pretty big deal for Swifton and he sat there so proudly.

As I approached him, he began to cry. Before I knew it, I felt tears running down both of my cheeks, too.

"What are we crying for?" I finally asked him. "This is what we wanted. We finally made it."

We visited for about an hour and covered so many memories. We talked about my early career when I first played in Swifton and Newport. We talked about how he used to drive up to St. Louis to watch me play when I was with the Tigers. It was such a special time for a father and his son to sit alone and share the joy of our dream come true. I don't remember all the things we talked about. One thing he said will always remain in my mind.

"I never did tell you this when you were growing up," he said, "but you were always a little better player than everybody else. That's why you're in the Hall of Fame."

That was the first time he ever said anything like that. I'll cherish those words forever. I thank The Lord for allowing my father to live long enough for that moment. Four years later, my dad passed away.

In my induction speech in August, I told the story of how my father raised three red-headed boys who he believed would play in the major leagues. Two of us made it.

When I mentioned that from the podium, some man in the audience with a booming voice shouted: "He was right...he was right."

My father watched that ceremony on television and I know he got a chuckle when he heard that man's voice.

I prepared that speech very carefully for a week. I wanted to make sure that everyone shared in the glory.

Kaline later told me he had sat next to DiMaggio on the stage.

"Boy, he can really make a speech, can't he?" DiMaggio said to Kaline.

I mentioned that my wife had no idea of what she was getting into when we married as teenagers so many years ago. Not once did she ever complain about the unusual lifestyle. Never was she anything but a rock of support.

My two children were too young to really remember their daddy playing ball. Most of their memories are of daddy being away from home so much.

I told them I hoped that this day would help to make it all worthwhile.

When I first walked on to that stage and looked at all those Hall of Famers sitting there I remember asking myself, "what am I doing here?"

After Commissioner Bowie Kuhn presented my plaque, suddenly I felt as if the time had come and that I truly did belong in the Hall of Fame.

And I knew it was a time to share.

CHAPTER TWENTY-NINE

AND SWIFTON'S STILL THE SAME

I t's a whole lot easier to handle recognition in a big city than it is in a town like Swifton.

There might be a few more little hassles in cities like Detroit or Boston for a recognized major league ball player or some other sort of celebrated person than there are in Swifton.

A player might be stopped for autographs. Or he may be pursued to make more public appearances than he wants. Those are relatively minor nuisances. They go with the territory of being a celebrity. How that player handles the situation is a measure of his courtesy. Once that meeting is finished, though, it's highly unlikely that any of the parties will ever see each other again.

It's a little bit different in a town like Swifton where everyone from the school custodian to the mayor knows all of my family and me, at least by name.

A lot of people here really don't know me as a personal friend. But because of the life I've led, everyone is at least aware of the success I've enjoyed. They know all of the places I've been, the people I've met and the things I've done. It might sound a little crazy, but that creates a little more pressure than what the average Swifton farmer probably feels.

I have tried to be a good person and a concerned citizen. I feel I owe that to my mother and father, my own family and all the folks around here who have chosen to make Swifton their home the same way I have.

I've always wanted to be well thought of in my hometown. For most folks, Swifton is only a drive through for a traveler on his way to Dallas or St. Louis. For me, it's everything I ever worked for.

Although I've never really left, it's a good feeling now to wake up almost every morning and know I'm going to be in Swifton or just down the highway in Little Rock every day.

After spending more than half a century in major league baseball in one job or another, I spent my first full summer in Swifton since when I was just a boy. Even though some things have changed, I loved that feeling of truly being home.

The smell of a cornfield after a badly needed summer storm . . . the whistle of that old freight train rumbling down those tracks that split the town . . . the sweat that soaks your shirt two minutes after you're out the door were memories I was able to happily relive every day. Even those pesky mosquitoes didn't seem to bother me as much as they used to.

There are certain things about the game that I still miss. Mostly it's all those fine people that I had been so blessed with for so many years.

Carolyn and I certainly keep busy, though. Late in the morning or early in the afternoon, I usually shoot down Highway 67 to visit George, Jr. and the boys at the motor company. Once in a while, someone at the shop will have a baseball or a picture or a bat for me to sign.

On my way back home, I normally drive around most of my farm land. I like to watch the progress and check to see what kind of equipment we may need.

I check out the land all around the town. Even the farms that belong to other people. If you grow up in farming, it's easy to tell which fields are being well tended and which ones need a lot more work.

I'm proud of my land. I no longer can physically farm it myself, but I sure do keep a check on all of it to make sure the people renting it are doing a proper job.

Summer evenings are particularly relaxing for Carolyn and me. With the satellite dish I had installed in my backyard several years ago, we can draw in at least three or four baseball games a night. We always watch the Tigers whenever they're on TV. Carolyn has gotten to know all of the players quite well. She knows when one of them has made a bad play and usually asks me to explain a little more about it.

I've got to be the biggest baseball fan in the whole state of Arkansas. Once the games are over, it's back to the books for both of us. We both still love to read and I take great pleasure in keeping up with any number of new historical or biographical works.

With the highway between Swifton and Jonesboro now paved as smooth as slate on a new billiard table, we can drive over to visit Terrie and her family sometimes three or four times a week.

Sometimes we just drive to Jonesboro for a night out at a restaurant. We've got a certain amount of freedom for which I must thank The Lord.

For those who've never lived in a town like Swifton, it might appear to be a little slower and lacking certain attractions that big cities offer. It is slower. We don't have a little shopping mall on every corner. And that's the way we love it. We can't think of another town in America where we'd rather spend the rest of our lives.

There are days when I drive over to the cemetery to say a few prayers for Charlene, my mother, my father and my brother, Frank.

Between making a certain amount of speeches and appearances at different parts of the country, along with tending to my farm land, I've got more than enough work to keep me busy all year long.

One stop we try to make every summer is the Hall of Fame induction weekend in Cooperstown. That's when the Hall of Fame welcomes in its new honorees and invites all members back to share in the celebration. There's not a time I go back that I still don't get goosebumps realizing my plaque will hang on the wall there for eternity.

The most important thing I have in Swifton is the church which has meant so much to me ever since I was just a boy. I'm very proud of the Swifton United Methodist Church. And I thank God every day that He has given me the strength to serve it the same way that my father did for so many years.

My father was so proud of each day I spent in the major leagues. I know there was no person on the face of the earth who felt prouder than he did when I was named to Baseball's Hall of Fame.

I also know that he would have traded all of those things for having me follow in his footsteps at his church. So I thank God that I never made him compromise any of his happiness for what he really wanted. I do share the same exact feelings that my father felt. I'm so proud I have been able to serve the church in the same manner as he did.

I've been extremely blessed by all the gifts I have received in my lifetime. I've also been extremely cautious not to take anything for granted.

When I played ball, I played each game as if it was going to be my last. When I was a broadcaster, I approached each game with the same   enthusiasm as I did a World Series.

It's still hard for me to believe that a little boy from Swifton could have seen all the things that I've seen and done all the things that I've done and then be able to appreciate them with his family back home where it all began.

There are still some days, late in the afternoon, when I drive by the park where the local American Legion team plays. Even when the diamonds are empty, sometimes I can see all those kids who played there so many years ago.

At times, I swear, I can hear my father's voice. He's speaking very calmly. I just sit there and smile.

"If they hit the ball to George, he simply catches it and throws the runner out."

GEORGE KELL REMARKS

At 44th Annual Baseball Hall of Fame
Induction Ceremonies
July 31, 1983

Thank you, Commissioner. I appreciate those remarks very much. My congratulations, too, to Si Burick and to Jack Brickhouse.

And my congratulations to Walter Alston. And best wishes to Walter for a speedy recovery. I know he's watching today. And I just want to say to Walter we miss you. We miss you very much.

My congratulations to Juan Marichal on this great day for him. And to Brooks Robinson, my congratulations. Brooks, my cohort on the baseball field ... today in the broadcast booth ... friend of many, many years.

I still find it, Brooks, almost unbelievable that we have traveled the same path for so long with the same goals in mind. And we wind up here in Cooperstown in the Hall of Fame on the same day.

Brooks, I know this, too—your friends, maybe hundreds, maybe thousands of your friends are here from Baltimore today. Let me share these friends with you for a moment because these people —I closed out my career in Baltimore an old aging ball player— and they were good to me. They were so good. And I share them with you here today.

When I was notified of my selection to the Hall of Fame, I received the most beautiful note you've ever seen from Hall of Famer Jocko Conlon. And this is what it said.

He said, "You never choked up on a baseball field in your life, but I'll guarantee you'll choke up at the induction ceremonies when you get to Cooperstown."

Well, it could be, but I hope not. But, Jocko, I agree with you. It's a very emotional moment for an old baseball player.

I stand here today in awe of this great event. I stand here today in awe of the great players that are behind me—the players that I'm joining, as Jack Brickhouse said, "in these hallowed halls."

You cannot possibly know the feeling that is inside of me unless you stood at this podium in this same situation.

I have suggested for a long time that George Kell has taken more from this great game than he would ever be able to put back. And now today, I know that I am more deeply in debt than ever before.

This is a very special moment. A very special moment for me and for my family. And we want to share it with everyone. Especially all of our friends who have kept the faith for lo these many years that one day this great honor would come our way.

I share this personally with my wife, Charlene, my wife of 42 years, who's right out in front. Charlene started with me at a very young age, as you might imagine, not knowing exactly what she was getting into, but not caring really if this is what I wanted to do.

I share this with my children—George, Jr., who's out here and Terrie out in front today. And my grandchildren who are seated there with them.

My children were not old enough to remember too much about their father playing ball. But they were old enough to know that their daddy was gone from home an awfully lot in those days. And I'm sorry for that. But I hope that in some small way that this day will make up for all of that.

I share this with my father—83 years young, who's in a nursing home in Newport, Arkansas today. Unable to be here but watching this on television.

My father raised three boys convinced that they would all be major league ball players if not Hall of Famers. Two of us did reach the major leagues. My brother, Skeeter, played for the Philadelphia A's—and myself. My other brother died in World War II, or who knows—my father might have been right. He might have had three major league baseball players.

Baseball has provided me with so much. Not just financial, but the people I've met and the friends I've made. Time does not permit me to mention all of those who have influenced my life. But let me tell you this. I played for Mr. Connie Mack and I got to know this grand old man rather well. I played for and I got to know Mr. Tom Yawkey, who left a lasting impression on this game. I spent the past 24 years broadcasting and working for Mr. John Fetzer, a real giant in the game today. There is no more respected man in baseball than Mr. Fetzer. I'm lucky to have played for and to have known these men.

Milton Richman, my good friend from the UPI, told me that being selected to the Hall of Fame would change my whole life. And it has, to a certain extent. But I would hope that I still know where the real values in life are. In home, in family, in church and in friends.

When I was leaving my hometown of Swifton, Arkansas, this week for Cooperstown, a 12-year-old lad and a neighbor of mine by the name of Ricky Roberts came up to me as I was packing my car.

He said, "Mr. Kell, we're proud of you. And we're all going to be watching you on television on Sunday."

Now I mention this because this touched me very much. I'm proud, too. I'm proud that I know people like Ricky Roberts. And I'm proud that I know and have many, many other friends.

So from the bottom of my heart, I say thank you to all of you.

WE'LL NEVER FORGET

As a young boy growing up only blocks away from old Briggs Stadium, I remember George Kell playing third base for the Tigers.

Playing ball in the neighborhood alleys or sometimes the park when we could sneak the diamond away from the older boys, everyone used to choose a favorite player that he pretended to be at least for that one day.

The best players on the Tigers always were picked quickly. Kell was one of the first to be chosen because every kid admired his rugged style of play. He always got the clutch hit. No one ever got a ball past him at third base.

Even after he was traded from the Tigers and younger players like Al Kaline and Harvey Kuenn came along, someone would always choose to be George Kell for the day.

That's the kind of impact as a player that he left on Detroit fans of all ages.

When he returned to Detroit as a broadcaster, I think most Tiger fans got the feeling that George had finally returned to the city where he truly belonged.

Having been raised in Detroit during those wonderful years when no one or nothing could challenge the fans' blind allegiance to the Tigers and all their players, I remember how George Kell always seemed like someone special.

He had come to Detroit from Swifton, Arkansas. He spoke directly and confidently with that little slow drawl that immediately marked him as an import to the automobile capital. Because of his courtesy and sincerity in everything he did, though, Detroiters immediately started a love affair with him that continues today more than half a century later.

That's a pretty good yardstick for the measure of the man. Kell performed in the two high profile arenas of baseball and broadcasting and never lost the allegiance of his fans.

George Kell had come from the South at a time when there existed a much more distinct cultural difference with large northern industrial cities like Detroit.

That didn't matter with George, though. Detroiters quickly embraced him as if he had been born in the middle of Woodward Avenue.

George always demonstrated a working-man's ethic. He approached playing and broadcasting with a blue-collar drive.

Even though Detroit sports fans are undying in their loyalty, they select their heroes with discrimination. A working-class city like Detroit demands honesty and hard work. That's why George Kell has always been a hero.

It's always been easy for fans to identify with George. And it was obvious from the start that George felt as comfortable in Detroit as he did with the boys from Swifton, many of whom had never been to a big city in their entire lives.

Even though I had been around the park on various occasions during summers while I worked for different newspapers in the Detroit area, I didn't actually meet George until 1973 when I became the baseball beat writer for *The Detroit News*.

George immediately made me feel as if we had been friends for all our lives. He didn't have to be so open. He already was on his way to the Hall of Fame and had established himself as one of the nation's leading broadcasters. I was a mere rookie greener than the infield grass.

But George knows no other way.

George is not the kind who preaches religion . . . he unashamedly lives an exemplary Christian life. His beliefs are vividly apparent in his actions toward others every day.

The ultimate measure of any man is the consistency he demonstrates. Not just over a period of days, but over a span of years and with all types of people.

For more than all of his Hall of Fame baseball accomplishments and for more than his equally brilliant broadcast career, that is how I will forever remember George Kell.

His principles have never wavered. His concern for treating all people with dignity has never been compromised.

George belongs to baseball history. He will forever be part of his beloved Swifton. Generations who grew up with him are grateful he became part of Detroit.

For so many who have been touched, not only by his professional brilliance but also by his genuine human concern, I thank George.

There are so many generations who will never forget.

—Dan Ewald

GEORGE CLYDE KELL

Born, August 23, 1922, at Swifton, Arkansas
Height, 5'-10". Weight, 170. Blue eyes and red hair
Throws and bats righthanded.
Married Charlene Felts, March 24, 1941
Hobby—Angus cattle
Attended Arkansas State College, one year.

Led all Organized Ball in batting, 1943. Tied major league record for most times facing pitcher, inning (3), seventh inning, June 18, 1943; hit for cycle, June 2, 1950; tied major league record by playing 157 games at third base, 1950; led American League third basemen in double plays, 1946-51.

Named by Baseball Writers' Association as third baseman on *The Sporting News* All-Star Major League Teams, 1946-47-49-51-52.

Year	Club	League	Pos.	G.	AB.	R.	H.	2B.	3B.	HR.	RBI.	B.A.	PO.	A.	E.	F.A.
1940	Newport	NE. Ark.	3B	48	169	14	27	2	3	0	14	.160	59	80	3	.979
1941	Newport	NE. A.	*3B-SS	118	462	71	*143	26	5	1	75	.310	148	*285	37	*.921
1942	Lancaster	Int.-St.	INF	127	465	56	139	18	2	0	30	.299	360	236	21	.966
1943	Lancaster	Int.-St.	3B	138	555	*120	*220	33	*23	5	79	*.396	*190	*362	23	*.960
1943	Philadelphia	Amer.	3B	1	5	1	1	0	1	0	1	.200	1	3	0	1.000
1944	Philadelphia	Amer.	3B	139	514	51	138	15	3	0	44	.268	167	289	20	.958
1945	Philadelphia	Amer.	3B	147	567	50	154	30	3	4	56	.272	*186	*345	20	*.964
1946	Phila. † -Detroit	Amer.	*3B-1B	131	521	70	168	25	10	4	52	.322	*143	*267	7	*.983
1947	Detroit	Amer.	3B	152	588	75	188	29	5	5	93	.320	167	*333	20	.962
1948	Detroit ‡	Amer.	3B	92	368	47	112	24	3	2	44	.304	108	146	8	.969
1949	Detroit	Amer.	3B	134	522	97	179	38	9	3	59	*.343	154	271	11	.975
1950	Detroit	Amer.	3B	*157	*641	114	*218	*56	6	8	101	.340	186	315	9	*.982
1951	Detroit	Amer.	3B	147	598	92	*191	*36	3	2	59	.319	175	*310	20	*.960
1952	Det. § -Boston	Amer.	3B	114	428	52	133	23	2	7	57	.311	113	216	14	.959
1953	Boston	Amer.	*3B-OF	134	460	68	141	41	2	12	73	.307	118	231	10	*.972
1954	Bos. x-Chicago	Amer.	IN-OF	97	326	40	90	13	0	5	58	.276	306	105	11	.974
1955	Chicago	Amer.	*3-1B-OF	128	429	44	134	24	1	8	81	.312	216	170	7	*.982
1956	Chi. y-Balt.	Amer.	*3B-1B	123	425	52	115	22	2	9	48	.271	138	198	7	*.980
	Major League Totals			1696	6392	853	1962	376	50	69	826	.307	2178	3199	164	.970

† Traded to Detroit Tigers for Outfielder Barney McCosky, May 18, 1946.

‡ Suffered fractured wrist when struck by ball pitched by Vic Raschi of New York Yankees, May 8, 1948, and was out of game until May 31; fractured lower jaw when struck by line drive off bat of Joe DiMaggio of New York Yankees, August 29, 1948; out for rest of season.

§ Traded to Boston Red Sox with Pitcher Paul (Dizzy) Trout. Shortstop Johnny Lipon and Outfielder Walter (Hoot) Evers for Pitcher Bill Wight, First Baseman Walter Dropo, Third Baseman Fred Hatfield, Shortstop Johnny Pesky and Outfielder Don Lenhardt, June 3, 1952.

x Traded to Chicago White Sox for Third Baseman Grady Hatton and $100,000, May 23, 1954.

y Traded to Baltimore Orioles with Pitchers Mike Fornieles and Connie Johnson and Outfielder Bob Nieman for Pitcher Jim Wilson and Outfielder Dave Philley. All players but Johnson were transferred May 21, 1956, Connie being added to trade May 24, 1956.

ALL-STAR GAME RECORD

Year	League	Pos.	AB	R.	H.	2B.	3B.	HR.	RBI.	B.A.	PO.	A.	E.	F.A.
1947	American	3B	4	0	0	0	0	0	0	.000	0	0	0	.000
1949	American	3B	3	2	2	0	0	0	0	.667	0	1	0	1.000
1950	American	3B	6	0	0	0	0	0	2	.000	2	4	0	1.000
1951	American	3B	3	1	1	0	0	1	1	.333	4	2	0	1.000
1953	American	PH	1	0	0	0	0	0	0	.000	0	0	0	.000
1956	American	3B	4	0	1	0	0	0	0	.250	0	1	0	1.000
All-Star Game Totals			21	3	4	0	0	1	3	.190	6	8	0	1.000